Good Local Wood

Keep the many values of our trees in the local community

By Jim Birkemeier

Copyright 2015 by Spring Green Timber Growers

Using **LOCAL** WOOD

IS

LOGICAL

A Really Good Idea

Good Local Wood – Table of Contents

All the benefits of using good local wood compared to choosing imported cheap stuff:

    using local wood keeps our money here, supports the local community, and creates good jobs

    using local wood directly lowers the demand to clear cut the tropics and Illegally log natural forests

Finished wood products are very valuable and should reward the grower and community for good effort

Good Local Wood gives a new alternative timber market for anyone who owns forests or has trees in their neighborhood. Promoting the use of locally grown and manufactured wood products is likely the biggest economic opportunity - right in front of our noses – today.

GLW Chapter One Good Local Wood – A Golden Opportunity

Most of the trees we see growing all around us today could be used to make beautiful, natural, high-value wood products, yet our local trees are basically neglected & wasted, while most of the wood products that we buy in our stores are now imported from another country. Forest management and timber harvesting in the traditional industrial forestry system is a nightmare for landowners and tree owners due to very low market prices for trees in the global economy.

We do have an alternative today in a new & separate wood products market - for the trees in our forests, yards, and along our streets - that can pay much higher prices to timber growers and wood workers while supporting the local economy. **Good Local Wood!**

Promoting the use of locally grown and manufactured wood products is likely the most potentially rewarding opportunity right in front of our eyes at this moment.

Our family forestry business at Timbergreen Farm in Wisconsin has learned to use **Good Local Wood** here at home to earn thousands of dollars per tree, keep the money in our local economy, put people to work with good jobs, and manage our forests for many wonderful values for our family & our community. We do woodworking and see our trees made into finished products and get to know our customers.

The best thing of all is to use your own trees to build your home and furnishings, the second best thing is to share your trees - as beautiful wood products with other people for their homes - and share their money.

We encourage our good trees to grow as long as they are healthy and vigorous. This large Red Oak tree today contains 500 board feet of high quality lumber that will earn us a minimum of $5,000 in product sales when it eventually dies from oak wilt. Most of the trees that we do choose to use earn us between $1,000 and $20,000 in product sales.

What we do at Timbergreen Farm

We encourage our forest to grow naturally, allowing and helping the good trees to live and regenerate as long as they are healthy and vigorous. When a tree dies, we may choose to carefully salvage the wood and sell beautiful high-value finished wood products to earn a profitable annual income.   We also work with our neighbors and local village to salvage good wood from some of the street and yard trees that are cut for various reasons. Our wood products sales now earn us thousands of dollars per salvaged tree, about one hundred times the value of the standing tree in the traditional timber markets. We put local people to work with rewarding jobs, earn full retail value for the wood in the trees we choose to use, and nearly all of the money stays right in our local economy.

We see our annual harvest of truly mature trees transformed into useful solid wood products that we sell direct to our customers around the world for full retail values. All of the many values of our trees and forests build and support our local community each year. We share what we have learned with other timber growers all over the world to continue to improve our forest management and wood products marketing systems, developing the best of the best ideas everywhere for our own advantage on our family farm.

The Terrible Traditional Timber Market

Our family has owned and managed timber for 47 years. At the start, we tried everything in the traditional forestry system. We harvested and sold timber to area commercial sawmills two times and found the results for a landowner and the forest were absolutely horrible. I would rather let my good timber rot away than give it to a rich timber industry that is plundering the planet and people for their own greed, offering to pay me pennies while they make dollars - while destroying our forestland as they take in the big personal profits with their global market dominance. Most people do give in to what they see and are told by the professional foresters on all levels – that 'it is good for society' to commercially harvest your timber, that is the market price, and it is better than nothing.

I Know there is something much better than 'better than nothing'.

We then learned to do just the opposite of what the professionals say, and now follow a new system we call Full Value Forestry – what every forest owner and forest manager really wants after all. We are in full control of our forest and earn an excellent annual income using just a small fraction of our annual growth. We are now applying similar ideas and methods to use the good wood in the trees from the streets of Spring Green and neighboring yards.

Spring Green widened East Jefferson St last fall, removing the large trees that were in the way of progress. The hired crew was just taking the wood to the dump, when I asked if we could use the logs. They then worked with us with good cooperation to salvage the value of the trees.

When a tree is harvested anywhere, it will eventually be purchased by customers somewhere as thousands of dollars worth of finished products – why not choose to do the manufacturing in the local community and keep the value in the local economy?

By eliminating all the middlemen and shipping costs, our prices for locally grown – finished wood products - are very competitive with matching global industrial products today.

These dead Red Oak are now truly mature. Oak Wilt and Dutch Elm Disease and windstorms got me into the wood products business and have sustained me every year for decades. Trees die naturally every year, why not cash in their value within the local economy?? Local trees can make thousands of beautiful, natural, solid wood products that last a lifetime. We sell first to local customers, but most of our wood is exported to population centers that need wood, importing their money back here.

The Essentials of Full Value Forestry:

FVF masters the Native American teaching of using just the dead and dying trees
   that the forest gives you each year - so the trees will last forever.
      Never allow industrial demand to determine what trees are taken.
   We let the good trees grow as long as they are healthy and vigorous.

FVF encourages natural succession and natural regeneration,
   Following the German Dauerwald teaching - "Watch Nature", we have the most natural and productive forest possible today

FVF carefully harvests an average of one tree per acre each year
      so the forest is never disturbed, changed, or damaged.   A small annual harvest creates a steady and profitable income

FVF practices Arthroscopic Logging to improve the forest
      skilled workers are paid an excellent wage for great work
      using the smallest equipment possible, doing the least damage and most good.

FVF utilizes each part of the tree for its highest value use!
   nearly every tree can be used to make something of value, it is our wood, we grew it, we don't want to waste it

FVF uses free natural wind power and solar heat to dry our lumber
      using Timbergreen Farm's unique Solar Cycle lumber dry kilns.
      The nightly moisture equalization period is the key to success that produces superior quality lumber.

FVF makes thousands of different high-value finished products,
   putting local people to work using salvaged dead and dying trees. Basic woodworking skills can produce high value products

FVF earns a minimum of $10,000 per thousand board feet for all species
   $10 per board foot pays a good wage and covers the costs, plus profit.
   The opportunity at this income level is to create one good job for every 10 acres of forest in this region, and for every 50 trees cut in one year in an urban forest.   Most of our products earn a much higher return per board foot of wood.

FVF sells wood products direct to customers all around the world
      usually earning full retail prices (but some wholesale is OK too) keeping nearly all of the money in the local economy.

FVF installs and finishes mixed species custom blended wood flooring, cabinets, stairways, furniture, etc. right in their customers' home. Nearly every species of tree can make high value products

FVF encourages other landowners and communities to earn
   and use the many values of Good Local Wood
   Forests should support the local community and economy
   the more people choose good local wood, the better for everyone

In the global industrial timber market, urban wood in a city or community will never have significant value as standing trees or logs delivered to a commercial sawmill. There is simply too much timber in the world market to justify using city trees as a marketable commodity – the costs are too high as are the risks. A large commercial timber company can not escape the global timber market.

A small local business can be successful with Good Wood

In a community that promotes the use of locally grown and manufactured wood products, there is a new and profitable alternative that is a game changer today. A small local business can be successful by not trying to compete in the traditional timber market, but be different.

Good Local Wood in Spring Green – Our New Plan

Every local tree that dies or is cut down for whatever reason - should be evaluated to determine if valuable wood products and/or fuel could be made from it. Half may not be worth doing much with for finished products, but for lots of them - for those trees that we choose to process - thousands of dollars per tree can be generated to build the local economy and put people to work with good jobs.

Even if we used just 10% of the trees now wasted, it would make a huge change – adding Billions in Dollars into the local economy and hundreds of Billions into the world market for wood products. Everyone would benefit except a few rich corporate execs, their friendly politicians, and those 'professionals' too lazy to learn something new & better..

There is plenty of opportunity for hundreds & thousands of new local wood businesses - every day hundreds and thousands of good useable trees are wasted in Wisconsin and more across the continent – only a few are used for high value products. In a new venture breaking into an old industrial market, strength in numbers is needed for small woodworking businesses to be successful. It is Go Time for Good Local Wood! First Come – First to Succeed!

Three Keys to Success to Using Local Trees

Good Local Wood in Spring Green WI has prospered by earning the full retail market values of three abundant types of trees that are not considered commercially valuable in the traditional timber markets;

- Small Diameter Logs – normally considered firewood, many small logs from 6" – 10"diameter can be sawmilled and processed into high value flooring and other finished wood products.
- All Species of Trees not considered valuable by industry can be salvaged and made into mixed species wood flooring and a thousand other valuable wood products.
- Curved, crooked, defective logs can be processed into high value products that use short pieces of lumber. Naturally shaped timbers can be used from whole trees in traditional construction uses. Specialty products can put more people to work.

No commercial sawmill or veneer buyer would touch the curved cherry log this board was cut from. We have learned to earn an excellent income from making high value products from these "commercially worthless" logs. $10,000 – $50,000 per thousand board feet is our goal to earn for this kiln dried flitch from a curved tree.

Use What You Have

Anyone can saw a good straight log, anyone can make money on a perfect prime export veneer log – we learned how to make good money from the rejects we were left with after the timber companies were gone; the small diameter, the crooked, the knotty logs - what we had to work with on our new family farm!! We learned to make more on the worthless stuff than my neighbors make from the timber industry on their prime export veneer log - if they ever get paid for one!! We occasionally work with a good log too, and make even more money. Earning the full value of the wood products in our trees - lets us take the time to do things right in our woods – as all forest owners and loggers and timber managers really want to do - if they only could.

This is not your traditional industrial use of wood

Our Wisconsin State Forester back in the late 1990s, Gene Francisco, told me after seeing our farm forestry business back then, "No commercial logger can harvest just one tree per acre, it is not possible." This is true, our single tree management system can not work in the traditional timber markets due to very low market prices for the logs. Commercial timber companies here must now compete in the global lumber market where most harvested trees are not even paid for.

Full Value Forestry is different. No State forester anywhere or any professional forester or college professor knows what we do today. Not one has visited in over a decade - or studied our current business – they are all totally afraid to learn about a landowner in Wisconsin being in full control of their own successful and profitable forestry business. They constantly make up excuses not to listen or look or learn, and actively discourage other forest owners from learning or doing what we do.

The latest example is a well-known forestry professor down in Indiana recently tried to rationalize that my business is only successful because we sell to the rich tourists that flock to Spring Green during the summer months. He says that our business could not possibly be successful in Indiana where economic conditions are not as good. He doesn't know anything about our business!

Gene also told me that the Wisconsin DNR Foresters would not pay attention to any of my ideas because I had an "attitude". This is a Very Common Excuse to avoid having to change for the better - still used today by all the professional foresters. Yes, this is true - I Do have an **attitude** – but there is no longer any excuse for ignorance today in the global information marketplace of the internet. Everyone; buyer seller, grower, harvester, forester, customer, leader, educator, seller – needs to know all of the available choices in forest management and wood products marketing to make a sound determination.

Street and yard trees also have not been harvested by traditional commercial logging companies due to low commodity prices for logs. One reason is they are scattered - one tree here and there is not efficient for a big business. Urban trees are generally poorer form, short, and open grown - compared to a taller tree from a forest. The biggest objection of all is that city trees are full of nails and screws and bolts and cables.

Metal In Wood is featured here

When I do hit a nail or fence wire in a log I'm sawmilling, I save that piece and use it for a special product that earns extra value for what others consider a disastrous defect.

WoodMizer sawmill blades today cost about $26 have heat-treaded teeth that can cut through a lot of old metal and still make me a good profit.

That is why I developed a new timber market for our scattered and commercially worthless trees that now earn us thousands of dollars per tree.   By eliminating all the middlemen, brokers, and shippers – we can earn full market value for the wood products in these trees and keep it all local. What we do is totally different and separate from anything and everything other professional foresters or timber companies talk about or do.   We capture the full value of the products from each tree and keep it local!

Using whole trees when building is a fad today in the USA, but when you travel the world, this is actually an old idea from simpler times. Here is a café in Thailand built with whole trees a hundred years ago.

Nothing suggested here is really new either, just old stuff that works - reinvented with a twist. The internet & global communications is now really a game changer – we better take advantage of the technology rather than becoming enslaved to other people who master the tools to fool us to get our money.

It is better than nothing

While my farming neighbors know everything about their corn & hay crops, beef & dairy businesses, they know very little about the most abundant agricultural crop in Wisconsin – Timber. Nearly half of our county and the State of Wisconsin is covered by forests. Farmers and forest owners ignore their trees as a profitable business, but have always taken what they can get for occasional timber harvests - as it is better than nothing.

My neighbor knows everything about alfalfa hay crops, how to grow them, when they are mature, how to harvest, how to use them, what they are worth, how much income they earn per acre from each step of production. He knows virtually nothing about his abundant timber crop – that is more productive and actually makes products that are more valuable.

Timber in this region is growing at about 25% of the potential due to repeated high-grade harvesting and neglect. The State of Wisconsin is getting about 25% of the potential benefit from our 16 million acres of natural forest and only a few percent of the potential benefits from our Urban forests.   Industrial logging is not working very well for the people or the forest here or anywhere on the Earth.   Only a few distant corporate bosses, their political friends, and some brokers - get rich from our trees.

It would not be tolerated by anyone if our Dairy, Beef, Corn, Alfalfa crops were managed this poorly.   No other agricultural crop pays the grower just a small fraction of the costs of owning land and production - while everyone else in the industry makes a good income with profit. No other major legal crop is grown and used to subsidize a hugely profitable industry, at the expense of the landowners and the resource. Yet the professional foresters say everything is just fine and dandy and sustainable in our woods, as this sustains their own personal paycheck.

The Country Today – Wisconsin's State Agricultural Newspaper:

Dick Hall writes a column, "From the Woodlot" twice a month as one of the more experienced and knowledgeable forest owners in Wisconsin. He has repeatedly documented that timber market prices never pay the forest owner enough to cover the costs of growing timber. He is committed to caring for his forest in the traditional system, and wrote in the June 3, 2015 edition "One thing is for certain, you cannot manage trees for profit in today's timber stumpage market, even with low management input expenditures. I will always manage for boards and cords but be prepared to pay the current and actual costs from other sources of income."

I have talked with landowners around the world for four decades about every aspect of the timber markets. The most experienced and knowledgeable landowner I have worked with has some of the best quality walnut after doing everything the foresters told him was good for decades. He shared with me that no matter how much money you get for your good trees, it is never worth the damage done to your land from the commercial logging operation. And he hates to see the good logs being shipped to the other side of the planet for cheap processing – but there is no alternative. Now that the owners are elderly and ready to quit, their children have no interest in keeping the land in the family and they can't sell the farm & receive fair compensation for all the work they have put into fostering a magnificent and productive walnut forest.

One of the very few people who I ever heard state that forest management was a profitable business was an N American investor speaking at the World Teak Conference in Bangkok in 2013. He presented that his group would obtain "just the very best lands" to plant Teak in Brazil. It had to be flat enough to do all the work by big machines. By displacing the native people from their best lands and managing a plantation for a while, they could yield a "return on investment" to some business investors thousands of miles away on another continent. (until the land was used up (or the market changed) and they would pull out their machines and abandon the land. Wood customers who buy cheap wood products support schemes like this all around the world.

My estimate of the average income people get from their trees in this region is about $20 per acre per year. This is less than the annual property tax. Talking with farmers and landowners, the consensus is that maybe if they were paid $200 per acre per year – they might then take an interest and learn about timber and manage it like their other crops. This will never happen within the tradition timber industry that has become globalized over the past few decades – the world Supply is greater than Demand.

For a major agricultural crop with very high values for the finished products, it is absurd that the timber growers are not paid a reasonable value for their harvested trees.

If someone blows a whistle in the forest – does anyone care?

While FIFA, CIA, NSA, VA, The Church, ….. etc, etc, all have been called out on the need to reform, update, follow their own rules & ethics - the even older more traditional & more secretive Timber Industry still silences the whistleblowers - and business as usual is sustained with lots of Greenwashing and advertising hype. Conflict of Interest, influence peddling, corruption, bribery, etc. etc….. is business as usual in most parts of industrial forestry, yet no one seems to care. Just my observation and opinion.

Rainforest Liquidators – the biggest wood flooring products corporation of all - has again been exposed for using wood from illegal logging and using the cheapest manufacturing methods, even though everyone knows of the poisons, all to save them money to be able to make the cheapest wood that customers choose.

We do Just the Opposite.

As a landowner and Timber Grower, I choose to be separate and work in a new timber market where the producer is in control and sells direct to the customers. With the new power of the internet, wood customers and small business can connect and find the values of Good Local Wood in new ways.

The advantage of a small business

Our family has taken full control of our own land – we know everything we need and want to know about how to grow trees and make wood products, and we can Google or Youtube or make a phone call to instantly get any more information that we need to learn these days. We love our farm, relish everything about being here & making our living here, and are free to enjoy it all. We learned how to stick it back to the big corporations – beat the rich guys at their own game and do it even better, right here at home as a small business!!

Today I Googled – 'Woodworkers in Vermont' – and found multiple listings of many dozens of small businesses offering good products and services to customers in that State – instantly!! Everything is in place today to gain the values of Good Local Wood and Food and Fuel! Wood products customers just have to choose to support small business and simply starve the huge monsters and things will change.

Trees are our most abundant agricultural crop

Trees are plants and can be simply managed like other agricultural plant crops. Our business success comes from doing a small harvest each year and earning a steady income. Trees are easier to manage than other annual crops as they grow over many years. If you work slowly, starting with the worst trees first, dealing with the most obvious problems, you can gradually improve a forest and learn as you go.

Spacing of trees is the main thing we manage, and is controlled by thinning. Weed control limits competition from unwanted species of plants. Let the good trees grow as long as they are healthy and vigorous! Simple! Start with this and learn a little more every year – You can See the Results Grow!

Here is how we do it today... at Timbergreen Farm

Full Value Forestry gives us a wonderful way of life here at Timbergreen Farm.   The most rewarding thing is to use trees that the experts and timber industry consider to be worthless or firewood, and make beautiful high value products, putting local people to work with good jobs, and earning full retail value from our customers. And it is really pretty simple and old fashioned and doable. We only salvage some of the trees that die and are available for harvest at this time.   Most are allowed to recycle naturally or can be used for fuel.   We have the option to hire more people to use more of our annual growth, if we could sell more wood products.

We Respect and Control Our Land

Respect is the ultimate product forest owners should grab and earn – We respect our land & forest, and we earn the respect of the customers that choose to buy our wood products. Respect is the key to our sustainable future, and is a result of controlling our land. No disrespect is allowed.

Other family wood products businesses have sprung up around the world following this idea. Small seems to be the key at this point as the huge timber industry and government forestry systems hinder anything larger from becoming established. There is a huge pressure to only allow industrial logging, and to make people feel good about the status quo by calling it Sustainable Forestry, Certified, Sound & Responsible. Influence peddling still rules if you allow it.

There is a new freedom today though, opened up by the internet, allowing a person or small business a chance to survive and even thrive in a global political market. The American Dream of a person working hard to become successful has now become the world dream, due to the new tools of the internet.

Most people tell me that there is no way they could ever do what I do. I challenge people to really learn about what I do before making that judgment – this is really not all that hard.

Anyone can today choose to learn and follow Full Value Forestry. You can begin today and build success day by day. A Strong Oak tree sprouts from an acorn.
A Giant Sequoia begins as a really tiny seed (left).
Starting small is how things work in the Timber Business.

A person, a family business, a small group of people in any community could produce Good Local Wood products from local trees; Natural forests, tree plantations, street & yards trees in a neighborhood. A variety of business organizations within a community are possible today to allow forest owners and neighborhoods to gain many benefits that are not available in traditional industrial forestry. Taking advantage of the many powers of the internet and adapting the best of the best ideas from around the planet is stressed in each aspect of the business.

Good Local Wood gives a new alternative timber market for anyone who owns forests or has trees in their neighborhood. Promoting the use of locally grown and manufactured wood products is likely the biggest economic opportunity - right in front of our noses – today. In Wisconsin, we could easily add $20 Billion per year to our economy if we used just 1/3 of the potential local trees. Twice that amount of wood is being wasted each year now.

The key is to stay small, keep as much local control as possible and keep the values in the community. We use as much as we can to meet local needs, then export our extra wood to population areas – importing their money into our local economy. A larger business won't stand to the global commodity markets for trees and logs and lumber.

My hope is that our leaders and all the professional foresters will soon realize that the big corporate approach to global forest management is not working well for the people or the forest or the planet, and accept that there is another way of doing things – promoting the use of locally grown and manufactured forest products. Maybe the whistleblowers will soon be heard and the traditional corruption exposed - to finally bring good forestry and fairness to our world.

If people are simply allowed to pursue this FVF in their community, instead of being discouraged and controlled and herded back into the flock, things could very quickly change. There really is no time to waste here for our leaders and teachers.

Be Prepared
I learned this 50 years ago in Boy Scouts – be able to be self sufficient.

Another reason to pay attention here is that at any second, our global communication system could crash. A major power failure today and everything comes to a fast halt - whether by nature or hacker – our modern lives are in total risk of instant calamity. The more self-sufficient we live in our community, the more secure we will be when something big happens. We all live like it will 'never happen to me', but we see it happening to other people every day now on TV. I choose to Be Prepared! I'm an Eagle Scout. For sure - have some food & water and a Generator & some gasoline for a few weeks on your own when something does actually happen to you and your area. (And a gun and some bullets.)

Finished wood products are very valuable and should reward the grower and community for good effort. The wood products from a good tree sell for many thousands of dollars per tree – the grower and local community can give the tree away for pennies on the dollar to a distant timber corporation to take this profit – or local people can choose to earn that money and keep the values in the local community.

Table One: Comparing Trees in the traditional timber market to Full Value Forestry

Type of tree	Value of Standing Tree	Value of Finished Products	Value Multiplied
Small Diameter Trees	10-20 cents per tree	$100 to $200	1,000 times
Non-demand species	$10 – 20 per tree	$1,000 to $2,000	100 times
Leaning Trees	$0 - loggers won't cut	$1,000 to $5,000	1,000+ times
Average Sawlog Tree	$20 – 60 per tree	$2,000 to $6,000	100 times
Good Sawlog Tree	$100 per tree	$3,000 to $8,000	30 – 80 times
Prime Veneer Tree	$3,000 to $8,000 each	$10,000 to $30,000	3-4 times

While percentage-wise, the small poor - quality trees have the biggest payout, the good trees are the easiest to process and earn the most profit overall. Use what you have – make stuff people buy - sell what you can make – that is what is sustainable - it is all good!

So, FVF has many values on many levels that people around the world can develop to build and protect their local community. We can show the basics and specific tricks we have learned here at Timbergreen Farm, but good ideas are best adapted to each person's advantage in their own home.

The ideas in good local wood apply to many other resources and businesses and communities.

While we work to develop the new market for local wood products, the Buy Local, Made in the USA, Grown and Made in Wisconsin, and Good Local Wood idea is catching on. There is a new hope for forest owners and communities with trees. I offer these ideas as nothing new – this is really just a return to simpler times, but using a little modern global communication technology to our advantage.

Some people need to learn everything for themselves - the hard way – one mistake after another...
   they eventually discover for themselves the ideas they once saw or heard and think they invented it
    maybe this hard way teaches humans so you appreciate and understand?

Some people take the best ideas they can find and make them even better for their own advantage

As a landowner, forest manager, professional forester, skilled timber feller, log hauler, sawmill owner, solar powered kiln operator, woodworker, flooring installer, wood products salesman, wholesale marketer, internet master, retail store owner, world traveller, Timber Grower – I see the how a new wood products market can work to make our planet a better place for our future.

This book is for both, but the second way is a lot easier.....

Good Local Wood encourages the forest owner to know and control their forests while earning a good income - using just the annual growth of the trees. Everything is based on the ability to earn several thousand dollars per tree per acre per year - so that it is worth the owner's time to invest and work in their woods.

The Best of the Best Ideas from around the world

Marshall Pecore, forest manager for the 220,000 acre Menominee Tribal Forest in NE Wisconsin, taught me on my first visit in 1997 to "Never let industry demand affect your decision to harvest a tree – only take what the forest gives you." My reaction at the time was 'nice idea, but you have to be practical...' We have since then learned to fulfill his teaching and now see the long lasting wisdom of this practice. Being a small business, and processing all of our wood into high value products, then selling direct to customers around the world, we can do a much better job than any big business or government program or University teaching or even the Menominee can do themselves.

The Menominee work through each forest management area with logging equipment every 13 years and make their harvesting decisions based on millennia of experience and wise speculation. On our farm, we can access any tree at any time to manage the forest for the specific conditions for every tree. This is way simpler and safer and more productive.

"Mature" tree is one of the most abused terms in the timber industry. So many rationalizations are used to cut that good tree right now – today – while the opportunity is best for the professional or logger or timber buyer. I've hear a million reasons to call a good tree 'mature'.

The only truly mature tree is a dead tree. Once a tree dies, usually we want to salvage it as soon as possible. Dead wood can be usable, but in our forest we try and salvage the dead trees the first year they die.

With oak, a standing dead tree may be usable for three to five years. Spalted maple may actually be more valuable after being dead several years. In Brazil, a tree may be down for decades and still be sound and produce valuable lumber products. If it is your tree, know what is still usable.

We have some flexibility, but normally we salvage, sawmill, dry, and use the wood from trees we choose – promptly. Use what you have!

Urban Trees bring many more options

The variety of trees in our cities, villages and yards is much higher than in the surrounding woods. People plant lots of stuff for many reasons, and things change more rapidly in our neighborhoods. Street trees often have lots of room to grow, so their size gets larger sooner. With more space to grow, height growth is usually limited, trees have shorter trunks, and their shapes are often quite round and wide. Despite these challenges – thousands of beautiful high value wood products can be made from Urban trees, offering many economic benefits and good job opportunities.

Rob Bjorkland near Santa Barbara CA USA is also following this idea. He said = "This is my Baskin and Robbins Floor" – 31 different species mixed into a delightful blend. Beautiful!

Trees along streets and in yards can grow exponentially in volume when they have plenty of room to grow. Trees often soon overtop houses and power lines, causing concerns not anticipated when the small trees were planted. Messy seed crops and fallen branches often irritate the homeowner, causing tree removals at any time. Urban wood moves faster than forest trees!

Rob has so many large high quality logs delivered and dropped off for free by the City and tree service businesses to his mountain side woodworking business (10 miles from the city) that he uses the extra logs to build terraces to create horizontal workspace. He and I both love to choose what good trees to process.

We should be using the better urban trees to make thousands of dollars of high value products, and convert all of the tree tops and branches and small trees not chosen - to be burned as renewable biofuel. An organized system could process the wide variety of products from normal removals and larger batches from storms.

Oak Wilt got me into the Wood Business!

I worked as a consulting forester for several years, beginning in 1976 right after graduation from the University of Wisconsin-Madison. Being the first forestry school graduate to go into business working with private woodlots owners in SW Wisconsin, I did not make the local sawmill industry very happy – (that experience is the topic of another book). After trying to implement the teachings of my college education and work in the government forestry programs, I quit in disgust – this system was clearly corrupt and very bad for the forest owners and the forest. I was devastated and discouraged.

Seeing the dozens of Red Oak trees dying of Oak Wilt each year on our own farm prompted me to start to use the wood instead of watching it go to waste. I began harvesting logs and took them to local sawmills to be made into lumber. Watching each sawyer work, I learned to make lumber from logs. Oak wilt got me into the sawmilling business and supplies me every year, along with trees killed by Dutch Elm Disease, and windstorms. Many more trees die every year in our woods that I can use.

I re-learned forestry from the forest owner's point of view, working in my family forestland. My guiding sense was "do just the opposite" of what the forestry profession had shown me was business as usual in the timber industry. Let all the good trees GROW! The "opposite" direction has been constantly leading towards Full Value Forestry.

Full Vigor Forestry

My first book, Full Vigor Forestry 2003, described our initial methods of growing a forest fully stocked with healthy and vigorous good crop trees, to produce the maximum quantity and quality of timber. The dead, dying, diseased, deformed, damaged, and doomed – The D Trees – are mature in Full Vigor.

Overcrowded trees that will all become stressed may be mature. The Menominee also teach to encourage the most volume growth with the most value growth while promoting the maximum natural diversity. This is accomplished by careful thinning of crowded trees.

Always start with the worst first – in any harvest, use the most mature. And pretty soon the worst is not all that bad. Worst First is only really sustainable if you learn to earn at least $10 per board foot for the wood products. This is the financial break even point for our business where a lot of hard work begins to pay off – from this point on we can enjoy the gravy from being creative.

This is totally Different – the Opposite of Business as Usual.

Indeed, the long term benefits for the forest owner and the forest - are just the opposite of the short term greed of big industrial forestry. I have no business contact with the forestry profession or timber industry today – we have developed a separate marketplace where we are free to do things for our own advantage. I am free to write this, where many others fear to say what they think or know to protect their job and paycheck.

After years of taking from the forest as a "professional" consulting forester - under the guise of sound forestry and collecting ridiculously high sales commissions on other landowner's timber sales – my thoughts and actions today are still making up for the errors of my youthful and naive start.

When we bought our sawmill back in 1988, I began to actually take the worst trees first – like every forester is supposed to – and learned to make money doing it! We let the good trees grow up instead of taking them down. Mixed species hardwood flooring and mixed species cutting boards & counter tops have been the main product that makes restoring the forest and harvesting the worst trees first a profitable business. Earning a profitable income from most tree species in our forest is a key to FVF.

Our biggest sellers are products that let us earn the same high price per board foot, whether Walnut, Cherry, Basswood, Oaks, Pine, Cedar, Elm, Ash.... The variety of colors and grain textures are amazing. Poison Ivy is the one species I don't try to make money from.

In the village and neighbor's yards, trees are cut for many reasons – often good healthy trees are taken for some decision, and it would be a shame to just waste the wood. Since many trees in urban areas are not part of a natural forest, but have been planted for some reason that no longer is the important factor, management planning is not such a long range issue. A future thinking community could encourage good timber growth for the many values and improve their urban forests as part of the planning and work!

The Key Three Types of Wood

Successfully using Good Local Wood is possible when you use three key opportunity sources of wood. As forest owners, we worked with what we had left in our woods after commercially logging had degraded the forest for over half a century. Small diameter trees, unwanted species, and curved trees were growing in our woods after all the large straight Oak trees were taken for "railroad ties".

 Small diameter logs make up most of the volume of the trees and commercially are considered just firewood or mulch.
All species of trees can be used to make high value products, not just a few species seen as having commercial value in the timber markets
Curved, crooked, short, and half rotten logs can be used by make high value products instead of throwing them into the landfill

The Supply of Local Wood is Great

Every day someone calls me and asks me to buy their tree or log or boards – the supply of local wood is huge and growing bigger everyday. We have to make the best decisions to use what we can – can't use it all but we could do a whole lot better than we are today. Each business or community can make a plan to use what they have and make things that are useful and sellable first locally, then in the global market.

We need people to call every day and want to buy our good local wood products. Maybe I should have named our store – Timber Sellers and not Timber Growers and the calls might be different.

People buying cheap imported stuff on sale to save a little money and hope for a better life are listening to the advertising lies of the big global corporations that keep getting richer from our collective local foolishness. I could sell a lot more wood products and put a lot more people to work if local customers would choose to buy good local wood for the benefit of everyone in our community.

Nature supplies us with piles of mature wood on regular intervals through violent storms. Most of this wood is wasted in the haste to restore power and clear roads and yards. If we used this wood wisely, lives and the community could be rebuilt with this wood, instead of simply paying to dispose of the misunderstood mess. More on storm salvage coming in later chapters.

Use it or Lose it

A storm took down one of my best trees. The walnut was split down the middle, then broken off sideways, leaving a real mess over our main ridge trail. I was able to salvage most of the trees value, cleared my trail, and minimized the mess from the damaged tree

There are many natural forests in parks and preserves that could easily use Full Value Forestry to benefit the local community. All trees eventually die and fall to the ground - using some of the wood has many benefits compared to the few mostly uninformed objections to Full Value Forestry. We only use a small fraction of the dead trees available, most do recycle and build the forest soils. I carefully consider every salvage for many reasons before cutting a tree down. Removing hazardous trees for safety reasons often makes sense here and in populated areas. Taking a tree down for salvage can be a lot less messy and dangerous than waiting for nature and gravity to prevail. And using local wood reduces the demand to clear cut the tropical rainforests – a very real reason to choose to use local wood.

Chapter Three Tending the Forest

Our forest covers over 200 acres and is expanding into abandoned pastures and field edges every year.   This is way too much area for me to keep up with – I get farther and farther behind what I think I should be doing all the time. 40 acres would seem to be much more manageable for a person.

Mark Havel of Willamina showed me this remaining remnant relic of thousand year old forest in a seascape of clear-cut industrial lands near Portland. A surveying discrepancy discouraged anyone from taking these trees to the mill, so they stand and lay today. Not what I expected, but a valuable lesson on nature.

After seeing old growth forests around the world, viewing natural areas that have been covered in trees for thousands of years, an old forest is a natural place – and is overcrowded and full of dead & down wood. I am now much more content allowing our family forest to approach old growth, than I ever was trying to simply produce more volume growth to sell to the timber industry.

Our goal today is to find a good balance between letting the forest grow old, overcrowded, and messy looking – and using some of the wood of the trees that have lost their life vigor or died or fell down to earn our living. When I salvage much of a dead tree, the mess of the fallen trunk and tree top is greatly reduced. I do much less damage to other standing trees when I fell a dead tree – my work usually tends to neaten up the forest's appearance. Compromise and Balance = working with nature and community.

Harvesting methods will be discussed in following chapters, here I will describe some of the things that we can do every time we walk in the woods and want to make a little progress at tending the forest. Often these things tend to distract me when salvaging wood as the need is ongoing and unending.

The German Teachings

A group of German foresters visited the USA in 2014 and picked our farm as their final visit to view our work that is fashioned after their favorite Dauerwald teachings.

When I first read Hans Schabel's description of the German Dauerwald forest management system, it was an amazing confirmation we were learning the right things for good forestry. And it is humbling to realize that our newest ideas here are just modifications of the old forestry that worked for the people long ago, before industrialization, mechanization, and globalization.

I met two other Germans who were visiting Wisconsin in the late 1990s, and got a personal tour in 2004 from Hans Klingelhoffer of the 33,000 acres in the State of Hessen, Germany that he managed. German forestry is "Another World" compared to industrial forestry in the USA.   They Value their Trees!

My favorite teachings from these Germans

that we adopt here are to Watch Nature, Encourage Natural Regeneration & Natural Succession, and tend the forest a little each year. Indeed another book of information is forthcoming on the German Dauerwald and Timbergreen Farm.

Tending the forest – For our Beneifit

Weeding, thinning, removing vines, and pruning are the basic tasks. If you can manage a garden or other farm crops, you can take care of a woodland too. Forestry is simple, start small and grow.

Do a little each year and there is little disturbance to the trees and the forest. Begin with the worst first – the highest priority work. Do the most obvious thing in this spot and then move on. Each time you pass through, the woods looks healthier and more productive. You get to know that place and the trees. Each year things get better and more satisfying and your knowledge and understanding grows too.

Be careful to avoid the forest management myths that support and legitimize industrial logging.

Everything about traditional forest management legitimizes the industrial practice of coming into an area with big machines and doing a large volume harvest – this is what makes the timber company the most profit. As landowners, we found that there is a much much much better way!

"Even-Aged" management is the most blatant tool "professionals" use to say that it is OK to clear cut a forest – taking everything in one pass (for the obvious profit of a big corporation).   This is profitable for the owner of the logging company, pays the landowner a little something one time, but leaves a scar on the land that takes centuries to mend. Clear Cutting a natural forest is Never The Right Thing To Do! Some even say it is Sustainable and Certified – Don't be fooled by the Liars.

The myth I was taught at the University of Wisconsin – Madison back in the 1970s - was that Red Oak, just like Douglas Fir out in the Pacific Northwest, and Southern Yellow Pine down in the Southeast, and other species around the world – can only be managed by clear cutting. Even aged management is 'needed' as the smaller trees mixed in the forest don't respond to thinning and full sunlight is needed for regeneration.   They do call it a B S Degree.

I believed this teaching for years until one day in the barn workshop in the 1980s, I saw this one particular red oak tree's response to the last big timber harvest on our land back in the 60s. Indeed, small trees can respond to thinning!! I've seen this growth pattern thousands of times since, though not one "professional forester" I showed it to would look at this and understand and accept this may be true. **So Scary!**

This part of a cross section shows that a Red Oak tree was 6" diameter at 80 years old and so extremely overcrowded that it was hardly growing at all anymore. After a harvest of the

surrounding larger trees – this suppressed little runt of a tree suddenly had sunlight & room to thrive, and began to grow with Full Vigor until the 22" diameter tree was killed by the Oak Wilt fungus - and then salvaged, sawmilled & processed. Seeing and Understanding this shattered my forestry education and training.

Better than Clear Cutting – Choose Selective

Selective harvesting and all-aged management = is the closest forestry teaching to that of Full Vigor forestry. Key improvements of Full Vigor is to do a small annual harvest and encourage the forest to be more diverse and natural. Selecting the one tree per acre that is the most mature for salvage is important. Earning thousands of dollars per tree is essential to doing that selective harvest in a careful and future oriented manner, with small equipment - that always improves the forest. Only the timber grower, the landowner has the real incentive to make the best decisions on what trees to leave to grow for the future.

Not all trees will become good crop trees, but certainly enough trees will grow larger to easily maintain an all aged natural forest with Full Vigor & Full Value Forestry. As I have travelled the world, thinning a forest and taking a small annual salvage harvest will work everywhere. The forest can actually support the local community if you don't just give it all away to a big distant corporation! The big old institution of the timber industry needs to be exposed for the ongoing corruption and greed that continues the destruction of our remaining natural forests while boasting about being sustainable, green, and certified.

Weeding – kill unwanted plants.

Invasive species are the most obvious to attack and remove. Every year there are more and more invasive plants to deal with and the fight can become overwhelming. Here we are lucky to have only a few Buckthorn, Russian Olive, and Honeysuckle that are killed on sight without mercy, but unlucky to have Garlic Mustard that has become established and spreads every year despite our major efforts to pull and spray them.

Killing native plants that we consider weeds is a little trickier. As a young forester, we killed off everything that wasn't Red Oak. Oak Only was the goal and was reinforced by the government cost-sharing programs. That backfired on us!

For years we slaughtered the Hickory as a weed tree that regenerated prolifically and persisted in the understory of the forest. Now the market has changed - Red Oak has dropped in value and demand while everyone now wants hickory. Foresters try to play God way too much, working to satisfy industry demand but not being able to see the future.

Eastern Red Cedar is generally seen as a weedy species that takes over now that the big fires have been stopped. We had killed them off for years, now we see that they are a valuable tree species and can be used for many beautiful products. Today we treat the Cedar as a top species – thinning and pruning the good trees and happily including them in our forest mix. The last time our State forester checked our Timber Stand Improvement work he saw us pruning Eastern Red Cedar trees and Freaked Out! He gave us the usual – "your work doesn't meet government specifications" and cut the cost-sharing payment in half. That was long ago and we haven't applied for any government money or help since. We don't need it!

Ironwood is another former enemy now considered a native treasure. My mind changed on this species in a barn full of wood slabs cut by a pair of prize winning furniture builders in Shelburne Vermont. Their favorite wood slabs of all - being saved for a very special project yet to be discovered, were large – thick Ironwood. We thin and release and prune our good Ironwood now, but don't tell the Wisconsin DNR foresters.

Prickly Ash is another native species that makes our brain and body struggle every time we walk through the forest. The wood is beautiful for turning and I make Prickly Ash Leaf Wine and even like the smell of the berries. We value all native species, though I still have an attitude toward Poison Ivy.

Box Elder is our most unwanted native tree and is often eliminated out of habit. We do have uses for the lumber and the burls can be exquisite, so even Box Elder can be profitable in our woods. When Lumberjack Mike and I have done training up at Winnipeg, Box Elder – or 'Manitoba Maple' - is often the best tree around. It can also make good syrup! Use What You Have!!

Choosing which species to allow to grow in your woods is more of an art than science. We would all do it differently. Being able to make a variety of high value products from all species and all sizes of trees makes encouraging diversity a profitable business. The cattle have been out of the woods here for 47 years and things are getting more natural every year. The trees are now regenerating at every opportunity, diversity is growing in our forest.

Thinning the Forest

Our forest is now getting very overcrowded – trees tend to fully occupy a site and become crowded in about 20-25 years. Density has a good effect of encouraging trees to grow taller and self-prune the lower branches, but overcrowding quickly leads to stagnation of growth. Timber Growers and tree owners should all measure the circumference of their special trees to see and appreciate how much they do grow each year.

One local newspaper story highlights this need: A large open grown Elm tree right along the street that everyone was familiar with - died and was cut down. An uninformed reporter quoted the older homeowner as stating as an amazing observation "That tree never grew any bigger in all these years." Anyone looking at the fresh cut stump would have observed the tree actually grew ½" diameter per year right up to the time the Dutch Elm Disease killed it.

I have visited Vashon Island in Puget Sound next to Seattle about every 5 years since 1974. As an occasional visitor, I see the incredible growth of their Douglas Fir forests and street trees, yet the residents miss the gradual changes and mostly waste the magnificent resource all around them.

If your goal is to produce the most volume growth per year, regular thinning is needed to keep the good trees growing. To grow, a tree needs a large leaf surface exposed to the sun, and lots of water. Spacing affects these factors directly.

Every time I cut down a tree of any size, for whatever reason, I take a quick look at the growth rings on the stump and take close note of the last rings put down. Read the story in the stump – the history of the tree is laid out before your eyes. Usually, the trees I cut show a slowing in growth the last years.

When thinning, I feel good when I cut a tree that has just about starved to death, but feel bad if I see the tree is still growing with vigor. I learn with each tree.

Trees that die of Oak Wilt often grow with full vigor right up to the last two weeks of life as the tree wilts off. The Oak Wilt fungus grows through the open pores of the Oak tree and plugs them, stopping the water flow in a matter of days. The tree is now mature – the forest is thinned naturally, my choice is whether to salvage the tree or let it recycle naturally.

My guide for thinning hardwoods is to take the total height of the tree and divide by three. This is the optimum spacing for Full Vigor Forestry. I don't work to attain that spacing right away, this is a long term goal that generally encourages us to keep thinning the crowded forest.

Spacing similar sized good trees at about one third of their height gives each tree enough room for a large leaf area to collect the sunlight.

Trees that are growing under the tops of larger trees can not get much sunlight. Some trees that need lots of sunlight – like Oak - will fade away, other more patient species like Maple and Ash can wait their turn for a much longer time to get into full sunlight. Deciding what to do with these trees is very difficult. Having a wood utilization system where we can salvage all size trees of any species at any time lets me give a tree the benefit of the doubt for another year.

Thinning is always done by taking the worst tree first – doing something simple – moving on and returning again next year to do a little more. Each year you know more about the forest and trees and the risk of making mistakes is low.

We can harvest small diameter logs and make flooring and food boards starting at about six inches in diameter, earning at least ten thousand dollars per thousand board feet. This is more money per board foot than a landowner can get from the one in a million "prime export veneer log".

We start earning good income from trees at a small size that industry considers extremely low value pulpwood. This makes plantation forestry, restoration forestry, urban forestry, and all forestry much more profitable and rewarding!

Removing Vines from Good Trees

Trees hate vines that climb up, hang on the tree, suck up water from the ground at the base of the tree, and shade out the leaves of the tree. When I walk in the woods, I can hear my trees calling out to 'get this thing off of me!' I hate vines, especially the ones on my good trees.

Wild Grape vines are the worst ones here. They overtop a tree and can starve it to death. While Grape is native and has a purpose in a natural forest, I cut it off my good trees when I work. Grapes are tough and don't die easily. I cut them off as high as possible so the loose end hangs above the ground so I can easily see it has been cut, and there is less likely a re-sprout or other vine will climb right back up. In a shady forest, cut grape vines usually die, but if there is adequate light, they spring right back to life and climb again!

Grapes are one of the few species I resort to using poison to kill them – Garlon is our choice. Spraying the lower bark of a vine with a back pack sprayer usually kills it and there is little overspray that affect other plants. Diluting with diesel fuel reduces the high cost of this herbicide.

Virginia Creeper vine is more common here, one occurring about every square foot of forest floor, but less aggressive, stays below the tree's leaf canopy, and is much easier to get off a tree. This vine hangs loosely to the trunk and is very brittle. I can always rescue a tree right on the spot, even without having a saw in my hands. These will try to re-climb a tree, but they are slow and don't worry me enough to try to poison the stumps.

Grape Vines and Virginia Creeper Vines have interesting wood that we can use to make money. Large grapes can be quartersawn to reveal beautiful grain patterns. Vines one inch diameter and larger can be turned for ornaments, tops, wood pens, etc.... Not even the wood identification experts have ever named the pens I showed them made from my vines! I have made $50 per lineal foot from vines! Indeed – wood products are very valuable in finished form!

Poison Ivy vines are common and I quickly kill any large vine I find. Poison Ivy clings to the tree trunk, has hairy attachments, and has large lateral branches with the 3 pointed shiny leaflets, flowers, & berries. Growing up in Scouts and in our woods, the plentiful stuff never bothered me. At age 39, while doing tornado salvage along the Wisconsin River, Poison Ivy vines on the logs caused an allergic reaction on my skin. Careful avoidance since then has prevented further irritation. To kill a Poison Ivy vine, I use the top of my chain saw bar to cut through the vine near the ground – throwing the chips away from me downwind. I cut through the vine twice and knock out the 2" long section so the vine cannot heal and regrow. They quickly wilt and die. Poison Ivy is the only forest species I don't try and make money from, though the green color of the vine is tempting...

Other vines here – Greenbrier, Bittersweet,.... are not much of a problem here at Timbergreen Farm.

Pruning lower branches—
Small dead branch stubs sticking out the side of my trees are a serious problem that is so easy to deal with – they bother me and I know that someday I will fell and process each of the good trees on my land.

Since I will be doing the harvesting work, pruning off the lower dead branches is a good thing for me to do today, while I am young and strong and the tree is in an upright position. If I don't prune my trees, I will have to do more work later when I'm older and the tree is now on the ground with many of the branches down in the dirt.

Pruning trees to sell to a timber company generally is a money losing proposition due to the low value of trees and logs as a commodity resource. Even in growing veneer quality walnut trees, pruning may pay off on maybe one in a thousand trees if everything goes right and the forest stays in the family for a long time.

My Rule of Thumb is to prune off the lower branches of a tree by the time they are the size of my thumb. Most trees I'm way too late, so I often do prune larger branches, but the motto is "Prune Soon". Usually, I'll prune off the lower branches as they die off, and occasionally take the next live branch. It the tree sprouts out of an epicormic bud, the tree is telling me I'm too aggressive.

Or a swipe with the pruning saw. If I get them off, these openings will quickly grow over with clear wood. These stubs left alone can persist for many many years and are an open pathway for insects and fungus to get right into the heart of my trees. Many times when sawmilling, I have traced a large rotten defect or carpenter ant colony right down to a small open dead branch.

My goal is to prune off all of the dead branches from my trees – doing a little more work every year. This is very beneficial since we will sawmill and manufacture the boards into products in our shop. Live branch knots are usually sound and solid 'good characters' that we use and show off in our wood flooring and other items. A dead branch that is long overgrown in the tree can produce a loose knot or hole – 'bad character' that causes multiple problems. Loose knots can be very hard and cause damage to our machinery and a hazard to our safety if they get thrown out while inside a planer. Loose knots and branch holes are generally not usable and that section of the board is cut out as waste.

Corrective pruning of walnut is a major chore. An insect kills the leader bud, causing a lateral bud to become the dominant growth leader. We often try to encourage a nice straight tree trunk, but with character wood projects, harvesting the special crotch wood, and whole tree architecture – we can use many trees considered worthless in traditional forestry.

The American system of sawmilling for grade is based on making clear cuttings of lumber from a board, eliminating all of the "defects" that often can add 'good character' that we use and show off. I was trained to sawmill for grade lumber but quickly learned it is foolish for a small business to try to compete with big American Industry. I found a better way.

Any time I have a chain saw in my hands in the forest, I'll do a quick tending project. A bad vine is an obvious start. Cut a weed tree or two, prune some dead branches, and thin a clump of trees that are way too close together.
There is always some good work to do. Time and energy is my limiting factor.

If I was bored and needed something to do – any time I can grab a tool and go to any place on our land and do some good tending work. These basic activities apply to all types of forests and any location.

We bought our farm 42 years ago. Over the years, especially when I was younger, I did go through most of the area several times - doing this work to restore some order to our woods after the severe harvesting and grazing that was common before we owned the land. Owning land for decades shows the good results from this type of work. Growing Timber is a Good Thing to do!

Tending a forest is a never ending story. This weeding and thinning and pruning is a lot of work and all of this only pays off if you are going to earn several thousands of dollars per tree.

If you aren't interested in having a profitable forestry business on our land, there is an understood/underlying idea in society that if you "own" land, you have a responsibility to do the right thing to foster the earth.   Before you subsidize the rich timber industry by giving them your good trees for way less than it costs you to own and manage your forest, realize that there actually is another way to do things that benefits the local community.

Forestry basics for Timber Growers

Protect the forest land from taking the good trees for short term greed.   Avoid harvesting that simply feeds the timber industry while not respecting the land, the landowner, or our future.

Avoid disturbing activities that will degrade the environment and pollute the water.

Work to eliminate or slow the spread of invasive species.

Prune the lower dead branches that you can easily reach. Dead branches are always bad – lower live branches can be pruned for personal preferences.

Thin out trees and saplings closer than 12 feet apart – that is just way too close.
  if you have a plantation
this is a basic responsibility if the trees were planted too close
  if you put 10 puppies in a box with only enough food for one dog –
    society and the media would expose you as evil!
  When thinning, watch the growth rate of the annual rings,
    or measure the diameter growth.
      Optimal growth is an annual ring of 1/8 to ¼ inch in middle latitudes.

      A spacing of about 1/3 the tree's total height is the goal we work toward
  Steady moderate growth is the goal, but we can work with anything.

Fast growing trees are really good when quartersawn
The looks and stability are great.
Slow growing trees usually have a more interesting grain pattern when flat sawn.
We use all trees and show off their individual character in a variety of products.

Every time I cut a tree down, I look at the growth rings and see how fast the tree has been growing.   Nearly all the living trees I cut show a slow growth rate from overcrowding.   Starting with the worst trees first, and doing a little each year is the key to success in forest management.

Tend your trees for the right reasons – growing trees for local benefits is good – don't just subsidize the timber industry because some professional forester says it the right thing to do.

Don't blindly feed industrial greed with your work, take pride in your work, do the right thing for our planet, build something of value for the community. We Manage our trees for the right reasons, to benefit our own business and local community. We know why we do things and how it makes our forest business better for our future.

Do Just The Opposite of What the Timber Industry wants you to do

 We Use what the professionals say are the disadvantages to growing treees (they take many years to "mature", dangerous to harvest, difficult to plan,….) to our advantage. We find the forest to be a wonderful place to live and work over the decades.

Most important lesson from college – one of the last moments in the hallway

One of the oldest profs – A cartoon on his door – for all to see

A logger in the PNW was felling a thousand year old Redwood tree with the rationalization

"It is OK, I'll plant another tree tomorrow"

Clear cutting and planting another seedling is not Forestry and not Sustainable – a lie to rationalize the industrial logging culture that makes the industry their money at the expense of the planet

Chapter 4 Trailblazing opens the forest

Walking through the woods on a somewhat level and mowed trail lets me enjoy the forest without having to watch and think about each step. Riding the ATV on our trail system allows me to inspect the whole farm in an hour when needed. I can salvage any tree any time and never take the tractors off of the trail system. Our trail system adds great value and usefulness to our land.

When I leave my woods trails and explore, a deer trail is often the next best choice. These large residents are like me – wanting to take the easiest path to get from one place to another – hitting the priority locations on the way. Deer normally take the best route and have even done some trail clearing for me. This works in reverse – the deer too choose to take advantage of my work and frequently use my trails for their travelling now.

When I build a new trail, following an animal path often offers good direction to start with.

Our woods trail system gives me easy access to every tree on the farm at any time the soils are firm. There are about 8 miles of trails through our 300 acre farm. It takes a lot of work to keep these cleared but the benefits are worth the efforts. I have a 165 foot long cable on my Farmi winch and I can reach any tree anytime without having to drive my tractor off of the trails.

Bulldozers

About the most fun I have had here were the three times I rented a bulldozer to build roads around Timbergreen Farm. It used to be simple to telephone the local farm implement dealer and have them drop off a bulldozer for a few days. For $35 per hour on the machine's meter, I had a blast building roads throughout the farm to be able to drive up and down from each valley and ridge top.

There were three short farm roads up to fields on our ridge tops that had been dug by hand long ago and travelled by horse teams until the fields were abandoned once the top soil was worn out and washed away. I dug in another 4 miles of woods road with the crawler tractors. Last time in 1996, I also did the major excavation of the three hillside terraces my log home sits in now.

Today, it is too expensive and complex and restricted for me to simply rent a bulldozer from current equipment companies. Every time I see an idle D4 Cat with a steerable blade just sitting somewhere, I want to rent it and make a few more roads. If you can get to use a bulldozer try it out! If not, work very closely with a local operator and machine if you need to dig in some trails on your land.

I only had to move a couple of medium sized trees and one rock, normally you can plan a route around and amongst the larger trees in a forest. One hundred yards an hour was my average production on side hill trails, a little slower going up and down the hills. I built in many water drainage features to protect my trails from washing away in heavy rain. Large, long, gradual side-sloping structures are better than an abrupt speed bump type water bar.

Make the trail a lot wider than you think you will need as they tend to shrink every year. The soil settles and the vegetation encroaches from all sides. I make a bulldozer trail 12 feet wide but keep the trees back even farther. Just cutting a trail with a chain saw, 8-10 feet wide is usually my first step, then mow and use the trails to keep them open.

Rye grass is the local recommendation for seeding down a newly made shady woods trail, though it is hard to maintain grass cover on a forest road. Avoiding using woods trails when they are muddy is important to maintain a grass and leaf cover to protect the soils.

Half of my trails did not need to be bulldozed to make them accessible by my other tractors, I simply cut the trees and shrubs and started mowing the paths every year.

Prickly ash, raspberries, and other brushy stuff takes over a trail if you don't use it and keep it clear. The roads I regularly travel with the big yellow forwarder stay possible with little extra work.

Roads less travelled need to be moved and the brush cut back. All trails have trees and limbs falling on them all the time – it is a lot of work to keep all 8 miles of trails here open for easy travel. Our mature fully stocked forest has about two tons of wood per acre each year that just falls to the ground naturally. I try to always carry a chain saw on the ATV and Tractors to clear the frequent roadblocks that occur regularly – and especially after a strong windstorm.

One benefit of good trails is that like the wildlife, even the flora and mushrooms likes my trails. In season, collecting food along the trails is a natural joy that makes the extra work of having trails pay off. Decades ago as I was just getting started, Mom realized that native wildflowers would become re-established in areas that I worked in. A little disturbance from doing woods work can have some good effects after 100 years of cattle grazing.

Once in a while, I clear a short side trail into a new area. We do everything we can to keep all of the machines on the established trails to leave nearly all of the forest area free from the compaction and disturbance of driving through the woods. I don't believe the story that a big logging machine only exerts a few pounds per square foot, so it is OK to take them into the forest. I wouldn't want a big logging machine to run over my leg and don't want one to run around in my woods.

Ecuador high line trail.

One project I visited on the Pacific side of the Andes in Ecuador, had built a 7 kilometer high line cable transportation system to avoid building a road to a remote forest property. Cables were strung from hilltop to high point, out of the forest, across the river – down to the nearest road. A Peterson Swing Blade sawmill was "flown" in by cable – and the boards were zip lined out to market. Here too, selling very high value wood products is the only way to justify the expense and extra effort of this high wire transportation system.

We had to hike on a newly cut trail up into the mountains – I suggested they improve the cable system for people passengers also. To get back to base camp, we hiked down trails through the rainforest that had been used by people for 10,000+ years. At river and creek crossings, the paths are sometimes worn and washed 20 feet deep into the banks. I felt a strong spirit presence on the hike back to the village we were based at. An awesome place that not too many Caucasian North Americans had ever walked.

Progress??

Footpaths that are replaced with a simple gravel road change the community instantly. 4X4 trucks and large trucks and then cars quickly bring new aspects of civilization to people formerly isolated and insulated from modern society. Logging quickly removes the forest to make way for food crops and progress, then cold beer deliveries, TV, power lines, and junk stores soon take over the once natural countryside.

I doubt that these people gain happiness from all the stuff roads bring in. As an Emergency Medical Responder here for 35 years, hearing all the suicide and overdose calls in my area – despite our major blessings of lots of money and stuff here, there are lots of

 very unhappy people all around me.

We invite our neighbors and friends to use our trails and enjoy our land. Horses and ATVs are welcome when the soils are firm, everyone respects the land following the lead of my parents. We lease the deer hunting rights and the trails are well used by all.

Easy access can sometimes lead to trouble, so proceed with caution and keep an eye open in the woods!

The most used tool in the world in the forest is a machete. This universal blade is used for many different tasks. Clearing excess vegetation in the jungle is my first thought, but people use the machete as an extension of their body all day long.

After a trip to Ecuador where we used machetes to make trails, harvest food, and mow the grass on the soccer field, I got one for my own forest. Our vegetation is tougher here – the simple slicing action of lush rainforest vegetation is not replicated with grape vines, prickly ash, and hardwood sprouts. But the machete can be a useful tool in North American forests also.

Cutting clinging vines like Virginia Creeper is a priority use that frees a tree from this pest. More careful aim to cut with the wood grain is helpful. Bending a hardwood stem to stress it can result in a cleaner cutting action. The back side of the blade can be used as a club for the dead branch stubs I dread to see in my woods.

A sturdy walking stick can be a valuable tool with many uses.   A club for dead stubs, a lever to break vines, and like a machete – a good stick is also a defensive weapon, though hopefully that use will never come into play. A few very simple tools can make a walk in the woods more productive.

Pruning Saws

Here is one of tool that professional foresters approve of for use by the typical landowner. They are commonly purchased, used a few minutes, and now mostly leaning against the back wall of the tool shed. If you are not going to sell high value finished products, you might as well save your money and energy, this workout is an exercise in futility when selling trees in the traditional market.

Since I will harvest these trees myself, and will make high value products in my workshop – pruning is a high priority for me. Pruning Pays off in many ways here, and is a never-ending project.

I have an arsenal of pruning saws. I should use them more. In theory you use them in a logical sequence, but in reality, they offer a nice variety of rewarding chores for all occasions.

Hand powered saws are the simplest – everyone should have one, whether you are a homeowner or a timber grower. If not for working in the forest, a hand powered saw can be used to trim up all sorts of trees in many situations. They are quiet = a very nice feature.

First you can have a small short straight saw on a handle that you carry in a holster on your belt. This keeps your hands free for walking and the light-weight saw is always handy for a quick cut. I can reach 6-7 feet high with this saw and get the first stage of pruning accomplished.

A three foot long hand saw can always be carried, used as a walking stick, serve as a club, and offer some personal protection. This saw reaches the second stage of pruning – up to 9 feet high - and empowers you to create a clear butt log on a tree. Any and every timber grower and home owner can and likely should work their good trees up to this point.

A pole saw is for the super enthusiastic person. The higher you prune, the more the work, the higher the danger, and the less benefits are achieved for the amount of effort. A six foot pruning saw reaches to 12 feet – a good level for hardwood trees, Any traditional manager of conifers – softwoods – evergreen trees, sees 17 feet high as the basic first goal. Traditional markets want a 16 foot clear log.

Motorized pole saws add the excitement of power tools to the pruning equation. In theory, the gas powered engine saves you work, but operating my extendable chain saw power pruner is the most difficult thing I have ever done around here. Arborists and power line crews do commonly use these for those hard to reach branches.

One place the powerful reach is a nice feature is clearing a trail of encroaching prickly ash or blackberries. I can cut off a prickly ash at a distance, so the thorny and angry shrub doesn't fall back on my arms and face and shred my flesh. Walking along and maintaining a trail with a power pruning saw can be a good use for this tool, and requires less strength than high limb pruning as the work is lower to the ground. Cutting grape vines is another job the extended reach with a small chair saw cutter head can be efficient. Cut the vine high off the ground where the diameter is smaller and prevent the sprouts from simply climbing right back up the vine into the tree top.

The extreme use of tree pruning – a friend used a tree climbing man and a 4wd man lift to prune his walnut trees to 40 feet high = the pinnacle of forest management efforts. But when this guy sold his best trees (for the good of society he was told by the foresters), the damage to the land was never worth the puny payment for the trees. And he hated to see the good logs exported to the Far East. His children have no interest in sustaining Dad's work in the woods. The farm is for sale, with no hope of earning the benefits for decades of forest management work. Traditional forestry and industrial logging is always disappointing to the timber grower, no matter how hard we try to do it right.

Prudent Pruning….

Dead branch stubs and dead branches should be removed from good trees for the long term health of the tree. Cleaning up a tree trunk while it is small – to minimize the work when you actually harvest the tree yourself in the future – is a wise use of time and energy. Pruning a tree to improve the quality of a log for sale in the traditional timber market is great exercise, but not a profitable use of your time. Pruning is most often an aesthetic thing, a work of art – you can change the shape of a tree from below. Kind of like Bonsai in reverse.

Every forest owner can make significant improvements with some pruning work.

Tree Planting Bar

I haven't wielded this tool for decades. When you let the good trees grow as long as they are healthy, they produce tons of seeds to regenerate the forest. Only when you cut down the good trees do you need to think about planting more seedlings.

This is another "approved" tool the experts say a forest owners can use. A lot of people plant trees in open areas that were naturally prairies here two hundred years ago. People plant a lot of trees that aren't natural to the spot.

Planting new trees to encourage diversity is an OK idea. In the Fall of 2013, there were huge crops of black walnut and white ash in certain areas. I picked seeds from good trees and scattered them in the forest in areas that were predominately red oak – hoping for a greater mix of species.

Don't trust cheap nursery stock. I choose local seeds from good trees that I know. Don't over plant – plan to take care of the young trees for a long time

If you have to plant trees, space the trees 12X12 feet with weed control and deer control. Use known good seed from a local super tree if possible. Prune the lower branches a little each year and begin profitable harvesting by age 15 at middle latitudes and after age 10 in the tropics. This is a short enough time for a forestry business starting from scratch.

Tree Tubes have been promoted for landowners for decades – supposed to protect and encourage hardwood seedling to get off to a great start. Great in theory but 99% of the tubes I have seen used were wasted effort. The investment will never pay off in the traditional market.

Collect seed/seedlings from the Super Trees in the forest – local good known genetics.

Most of the trees that I have seen planted in this region were put in the ground way too close and never taken care of, creating a mess for any thought of a profitable business.

Dead beat forester owners – it is easy to make babies, but a lot of work to take care of them over the years.

Be prepared to tend the forest a little every year – forever. Planting trees is a big responsibility. Start pruning as the trees become crowded and do a little each year. One or two lower branches a year works here on many types of trees.

Puppies in a box – it always makes the news when people neglect animals. Trees are alive too and should be cared for.

Trees know how to propagate if people don't mess it all up – we mostly have too many trees already in our forest.

Plan to start making money when the trees are 6 inch diameter – 15 years here 5 -10 years in the tropics and grow on that every year

Water Bottle

Carrying a little water extends the time I can spend in the woods. Once you start doing stuff, thirst can quickly surface, tempting you to head back to the chair on the deck to simply look out at the forest. One water bottle often doubles the amount of work I can do in a session. A recycled pop container filled with my wonderful well water is my companion all summer – maybe a half dozen on a hot day.

Chain Saws

Kind of like guns, people own a lot of chain saws. A friend has a gun of every caliber, I have a chain saw of each bar length and cc.

Likely the most dangerous thing anyone does in the woods, working with chain saws is pretty scary.

Sharpening the chain of cutters is the most important skill. A chain saw chain should be fine tuned to feed into the wood at the rate the engine can supply the power. You should never force or lever the cutting bar through the wood - be sharp and stay sharp!

Never work when you are tired. When you are making good money from each tree, you never have to push for production and volume. Make valuable products and enjoy your time in the woods.

Kick back – hope the chain break works or you are in trouble. Kick back is usually so fast, you can't control it. My chain break is my best friend in the woods.

Chaps and pants Really good for prickly ash and black berries, but not much help for a sharp professional chain saw. May give you a little warning and slack Too hot for me most of the year. Don't work when it is too cold anyway. The key to chain sawing it to be totally afraid and respectful and always pay attention to everything. No safety equipment protects against carelessness or ignorance.

Gloves & Glasses

Year round, it is wise to always have a pair of work gloves – the forest is a sharp, rough, and pointy place. Safety glasses can save a lot of pain and suffering - find a balance between too much stuff and being in nature.

Falling trees –A risk we take every day is that trees and branches fall everyday in all weather. An average of over 2 tons of timber fall in each acre of our forest during a year. Roll bars and steel cages and hard hats offer a little protection, but always be ready to duck and run. Don't bump into old dead standing trees, bigtooth aspen are the worst risk here. Even though I hug me trees all the time, they are always trying to kill me and work together at times. Walking in the woods is still less deadly than driving into town, but beware as trees fall everyday.

Cell phone – a new excuse to be irresponsible and work in the woods by yourself. I use it a lot. Working alone in the woods has its advantages, but the old teaching to never work alone in the woods has its reasons. I never go out into the forest without my cell phone.

Working in the woods is very rewarding and can be a very spiritual experience. Quiet time helps connect to the forest and trees.

This is Pete, the proud owner of a brand new Ponsse harvester (made in Finland) – working today in the River Valley School Forest near Spring Green. The protective mat was still on the floor and the clear plastic seat protector still in the cab – and it had that new harvester smell inside.

8 Wheel Drive – 330HP Mercedes Diesel Engine - State of the Art computers – 33 foot reach, Best ever, here in Wisconsin and the world.

Pete is from Northern Wisconsin – started cutting timber at age 18 – now owns his business. His computer screen/hydraulic operated chain saw cuts timber to 1/32" tolerance. He was cutting and sorting hardwood pulpwood, red pine pulpwood that will be hauled 100 miles to Wisconsin Rapids, sawlogs for three different sawmills up north (200 miles haul) and the best red pine were cut for utility poles for a preservative treating plant in N Wisconsin. Most of the wood will be 2X4s and power poles, with the small stuff heading for the chippers.

None of the wood will be used around here, Pete told me.

A timber buyer from the pole plant up North marked this red pine tree with the length of pole, the red paint number showing Pete how to cut the most valuable product from this harvest.

I learned all about the current State of our State's timber industry today from a fellow logger – eager to learn what we do down here.

We had a great time sharing our experiences as he worked
from our two different worlds working in the woods of Wisconsin:

Pete has the most expensive and powerful machine possible	I have a chain saw I carry by hands
Pete has to produce hundreds of cords of wood each day	I cut a tree once in a while
Pete is working 200 miles from home	I walk 100 yards down to my sawmill and shop
Pete has to work 16 hours a day to make his payments	I have no payments to the bank and work when I want to
Pete is safe and comfy and warm in his captain's chair	I work within nature in my woods
Pete never sees the wood once the trucks leaves the site	I make finished products that I install in my customers home
Pete's logs will be hauled by big trucks many times work	I take my wood products to the customer in my truck on my way to
Pete earns a dollar or two per tree	I earn thousands of dollars per tree
Pete is unsure of the future of this forest after he is gone	I know my forest will improve every year as I work
Pete works really hard for a living	I live for my work in my family forest

Spring Green receives little benefit from this harvest   **80% of the value of my salvage harvests stays in the local economy**

I could write a whole book – but you get the gist....

Pete is the poster child for the Traditional Timber Industry   I know there is another way that has many benefits everyone wishes for

Here I'm sawmilling a six inch diameter 42 year old red pine, salvaged from the hillside above me home. This tree was about dead from over crowding, but we will use this pole for a building project. Using your own wood is the best thing, but selling it in the local community is second best.

We use the best machines and the best ideas to get the most value possible from the trees in our forest. The possibilities are endless, only limited by a person's imagination.

Chapter Six Felling Timber

Hearing the crack as the last fiber holding a standing tree vertical breaks, then the crash of the tree hitting the ground is the peak of excitement in Full Value Forestry. The danger, the action, the challenge to do it in the best possible way keeps me going.

Forest owners are told by the experts that it is too dangerous for them to cut down big trees. I admit that I'm lucky to be alive considering all the tree felling I did before good training was made available to me. Now, the risk is a reasonable part of the business with good training.

I use the Swedish style – Shallow Face Notch Bore Cut Method – taught by Soren Erickson and continued by the Game of Logging and Forest Industry Safety Training Alliance and others. I took the first two sessions of Game of Logging, but have watched Lumberjack Mike fell timber for decades now. Our favorite feller learned directly from Soren on the Menominee Tribal Forests long before this fellow ever ventured South to work with us here in Spring Green.

Safety is one important reason to use this method. The key is that you can do 98% of the work of felling the tree, and the tree doesn't move at all until you are ready to cut the last fiber and run to a safe location. Most fellows falling trees do the 45 degree wedge cut in front, then cut in from the back until the tree goes down. A back cut slices through the back-side fibers right away that are holding up the tree, and the tree starts to fall and move and lean and crack - causing a variety of serious problems. Falling branches and splitting up the middle creating a "barber chair" can be fatal to the person making the traditional back cut when felling a tree.

Minimizing the splits in the valuable butt log of the tree is another important and more commonly appreciated reason to perfect this method of cutting down a tree. Only when you make the chain saw cuts, then follow through the steps of sawmilling, kiln drying, manufacturing, and finishing – can a person see the whole picture of harvesting a tree and working the wood. To know this is pretty unique in the timber industry today. Being in control of this is a rewarding feeling.

When I get dry lumber out of the kiln, it is really rewarding to see all these wonderful boards that were made from dead and commercially worthless trees. This is the time I can actually see how good a job I did when felling and bucking the tree into logs. Every tiny split in the log is now seen clearly in the boards. Many splits in the dry lumber were not noticeable in the fresh cut log or green lumber.

Salvaging trees in the cities, villages, yards, and along roads could be improved with this training. I get trees from all kinds of professional crews who have had chain saw and safety training in their jobs. Many have decades of experience, but their training and emphasis is getting the tree down fast with minimal expense.

I believe most workers would appreciate good training on how to produce high value products from these trees. No one enjoys seeing trees go to waste. People feel a sorrow for killing live trees.

Creating higher value logs should be rewarded with better pay for the workers. Everyone should benefit from using local trees – the wood products are very valuable.

The Village of Spring Green has dozens of Ash and Maple dying at this time. We have a plan for the next salvage that will improve on the last two projects we have already accomplished.

Trees will be marked for removal and interested businesses notified of the salvage. I can inspect the trees and choose which ones are worth our while to process into products. Any specific situation can be planned for and dealt with.

If a tree can be simply and safely felled, then cut into logs and the tops cleaned up – we will work directly with the village crew, saving the taxpayers money with our efforts. We can control the process and make the best of the tree's value.

If a tree needs to have the tree top removed before felling the trunk, a tree service crew will come in and do that work, leaving the butt log stand. Our crew will then carefully fell the log and remove the wood. Again, our business will get some good wood and the taxpayers will save money. We will also employ local workers to make and sell wood products, adding several thousand dollars per tree to the local economy. Everyone feels better when a tree that had died or must be removed is made into a long lasting useful product.

A training program for salvaging trees for making high value products could be made available to tree service, power line, public workers before the next big storm hits, so that everyone knows how to get the most use out of storm damaged trees. Vacant lots should be designated for log drop off spots so that the wood can be stored until the logs can be sawmilled into lumber.

This method is too complex for me to attempt teach in this book, but hopefully these reasons will encourage you to watch videos and research the method and take some training. The more you do this, the better you get. I'm still learning and improving – I love the challenge of trying to cut the perfect log.

When I fell a tree, I'm never in a hurry. I can take my time and enjoy the process. Knowing that this tree will earn me thousands of dollars gives me the freedom to do things the best way possible. Knowing that all the other trees in the area also have high value, makes me very careful not to damage them. Knowing that I will be back here to this spot every year to do more work helps me do the right thing for the future.

The spirit of the forest = trees are alive here – a living community. Get to know the spirit of each area of the forest.

You can hug trees over and over but once you pick up a chain saw they will all work together to try to kill you too. Tag Team Trees have scared me many times. Know that the trees will try to kill you and they work together. No matter how often you hug your trees, Never turn your back without covering your backside.

And hope for good luck too – you never know what will fall at any second = that is living in the forest. Two Tons of Trees Per Acre Per Year fall to the forest floor every year in our woods. Just the way it is – just hope that it will never happen to you and Go For It

I try to take a spotter to watch me when I cut down a large tree, so see the things from a different point of view. I watched Lumberjack Mike for years, and his Uncle Bob for years before that, and dozens of loggers doing it all different ways before that. Now I show the younger folks what I can while I still can. At 62 years old with 40 years of tree harvesting experience, I'm getting better each day! Anyone can clear cut with a big machine. Harvesting one tree per acre takes training, skill, practice, patience and can be paid for by selling high value products from the tree.

The satisfaction of carefully salvaging a dead tree and putting local people to work making long lasting beautiful home furnishings is Great!

Arthroscopic Logging

An orthopedic surgeon watching our logging demonstrations commented that what we do reminds him of Arthroscopic Surgery. "You make the smallest possible incision, use the smallest tools possible, do the needed work, you leave the patient better than when you started, and the subject is able to immediately move on and grow better." This is not possible in the traditional timber industry market, only if you earn very high values for your harvested trees can you spend the time and effort to do things right when logging. If you are not earning thousands of dollars per tree, there is no way you can do what we do here at Timbergreen Farm.

As a Boy Scout I learned to camp and live in the woods of S Wisconsin. Our troop avoided established campgrounds and loved to back pack to a primitive camp in natural areas – one of our favorite places was a natural wooded farm in the Baraboo Hills. At 13 years old, I guided my patrol through the forest following our map and compass to a hilltop stand of oak trees for our annual adventure. We were all suddenly stunned – the map said we had arrived, but no one could recognize our familiar campsite – the forest had been taken and a huge mess of tree tops and rutted ground was all we saw. That day changed my life – it was so obviously a violent cutting of this once beautiful forest that damaged the land in so many ways.   We did have plenty of easy firewood for our campfire.

My love for the woods encouraged me to go to Forestry School and go into business as a forester working with the farmers in SW Wisconsin. I learned every part of the timber industry and as a young naïve activist, worked to do things right in the midst of a very traditional business. I soon got really bummed out.

The timber industry is a huge thing – a Trillion dollars a year dynamo. It is what is it today, but from the forest owners point of view, there is nothing good about it, especially when claims of "sustainability" and "sound forestry" and "certified eco-friendly" are used everyday.   No one alive today was even born when the current institution was developed – but we are all responsible for what we do and there is no longer any excuse for ignorance – everything is seen and known today. We can all choose to do better now with what we know today.

The Worst of the Worst

Transporting Logs through the forest is likely the most damaging part of commercial logging. Tree length skidding is the worst practice I that have I have seen in 50 years watching the timber industry around the world – but there are no good practices in industrial logging .   Moving heavy volumes of logs has major impacts no matter how you do it.

I am a logger, I know the business – I rarely criticize a logger – they are usually doing the best they can in the situation that they are in. The crew doing the woods work is the deciding factor on how the forest is treated, each action has an effect that lasts decades and centuries. A good crew is really important.

Earning enough money to pay a professional timber harvester to perform excellent logging during a small annual harvest was the initial incentive to developing the Full Value Forestry system. Later we added the notion that the forest owner and local community should also be paid a fair and profitable income for their time, effort, and investment.

I use the small possible equipment to minimize damage while moving tons of wood. Having a good trail system is the key to success in any forest management operation. Do a little at a time to minimize damage and maximize the benefits to the forest.

You simply have to sell high value products to make small scale local timber harvesting/salvaging in natural forests, tree plantations, restoration forestry, and now Urban forestry - profitable/practical/sustainable – there is no compromise anywhere that works.

White Oak Tree Salvage

The leaves have just come out of their buds (it is May at Timbergreen Farm) and it is again obvious if a tree is dead or dying. A nice two foot diameter White Oak was spotted right along a ridge trail, bare of leaves – killed by Oak Wilt and mature. The tree has a definite lean directly toward another good live White Oak. To salvage the high quality lumber before it stood another summer, I felled the tree in the one spot possible without damaging any other trees. The logs were picked up with the prehauler and carried ¼ mile down to the sawmill.

This 24" DBH tree was 150 years old, has 4 eight foot long logs in the trunk and was estimated at about 360 bf with the Scribner Tree Scale. The actual logs cut were tallied at 420 board feet. This tree represents the average annual growth per acre at Timbergreen. By carefully felling the tree, no damage was done to other trees. Using most of the wood for logs and firewood left just a very low stump and a small bunch of upper limbs - to recycle into the forest floor. As I worked, I pruned several young trees, cut a large vine from another tree – I always do some improvement work every time I have a chain saw in my hands. This one dead tree should earn us about $5,000 in wood product sales.

Logging on Frozen Ground

Here in Wisconsin where we have specific seasons with very different logging conditions, the foresters say you should only cut Oak timber when the trees are dormant, the oak wilt fungus is not present, and the ground is firm or frozen. That is where I started out, and all my early teachings and writings told the landowners to only allow commercial logging during optimum frozen conditions to protect your land and standing trees.

After travelling around the world a few times and living & working with farmers deep in the tropical rainforests, that teaching doesn't make any sense to most timber growers. Luckily – all of the Arthroscopic Logging techniques we use here now, also do work well in the rainforest and anywhere else in the world. Careful directional felling, using the smallest equipment possible (Arches, Winches, ATVs, trailers….) , having the best tool for each logging situation is the best timber harvesting system in the world.

The real key is respecting the forest and the land and the future. I have seen big skidder operators who respect the land and can do excellent work with a big machine – it is possible if the worker cares and is paid well to do excellent work. Valuing the future production of the forest is the mindset everyone must have to do things right. No compromise and no conflict of interest.

Paying a logger well to do professional work is the foundation of all of our work. A forest manager can do nothing without an excellent worker in the woods, and this applies where I do both myself also.

Horse skidding

Pulling logs out of the woods is an old method that people still love today. In 1997, our Timbergreen Farm training program got a huge boost from the Wisconsin State Journal featuring our Amish horse logging on the front page. Over the next two weeks, hundreds of landowners came to see our demonstrations. The famous but fatally flawed Sustainable Woods Cooperative movement quickly came from this mass of forest owners.

I foolishly challenged one horse to a skidding contest with my 300 cc Honda ATV. No contest – the horse had way more pull.

In an open forest, two horses have room to maneuver and can be very effective at moving logs. A two horse team is often bulky and cumbersome and clumsy in a full stocked forest. Again, having the best set up for each situation is really important.

Pulling down the hill is always a good thing when moving heavy logs with small equipment. Gravity is a very serious force that must be dealt with. If icy or muddy ground is underfoot, going downhill can be dangerous and skidding is exciting due to lacking control of much of anything. Still, most seem to choose working with gravity and hoping for good luck.

The best use of horses I have experienced is in large forest areas with no trail system. One horse can move small batches of logs down to the edge of the woods very effectively. This is perfect for an annual harvest of scattered logs from a roadless forest.

You have to love working with animals to do horse logging.

People power

Moving wood out by hand is practical for small amounts of high value products. Some folks find the exercise and experience of working in the woods adequate compensation for doing things by hand and back. Burls, mushrooms, maple sap, wild game have all been hauled manually around here over the years.

Long before digital cameras, one image still etched in my mind is Wisconsin Badger Linebacker Gary Buss backpacking a huge red oak burl from the back 40 out to the road. He loved the challenge & workout, and there was no alternative to salvage that unique piece of timber that day.

Winches

Our Farmi Winch has been extremely useful over the years – a very versatile tool for all kinds of work. 10,000 pounds of pull is barely enough to move heavy logs – you have to be smart and resourceful, compared to a large industrial logging machine that simply uses brute force to rip logs from the forest. We can use pulleys to change the direction of the pull, or double the pulling force when needed.

Care of the mainline cable is important – we are still using the original cable after 40 years. Having a good slip clutch to prevent damage is good.

I also keep the tractor engine speed on idle to reduce the risk of danger or damage in tricky skidding operations.

Changing direction of the pull using pulleys is very helpful and often essential when skidding logs through the woods and up the steep hills of our land. It seems the load always heads directly for the closest stump, rock, or standing tree.

Radio control has added a new value to the winch and makes me more independent when working. The old way was to use walkie talkies so I could tell the winch operator at the top of the hill when to pull and when to stop. Now a push button in my hand simply controls the pull for me as I walk back in with the log. Planning ahead and antici – pation keep this hard job challenging and interesting.

The combination of a pulley, nylon strap, and radio control lets me winch logs to the trail with good speed.

Winching a log on the ground takes a lot of power, digs up the dirt, and gets the log's bark packed full of abrasive debris that dulls the sawmill blade. Sometimes we still choose to just drag a log through the dirt, but only as a last resort if no other better solution is available.

A small gasoline powered capstan winch and a small arch may be the lowest impact mechanical logging system of all. We use the smallest tool that is reasonable for each job.

Horses, Winches, manual moving of logs require careful planning and the ability to make high value products from the logs, to make these methods feasible and profitable. We work hard and produce high value for our wood, we never just try to produce large volumes of wood. We never want to compete with big industrial logging and sawmilling operations.
We have to be much smarter.

ATVs

I love to drive around on my Honda ATV. With 300 acres of hilly land to work, at this age an ATV is quite a machine. My main reason (excuse) for riding around most of the time is that I am a volunteer Fire/ Rescue responder with the Spring Green Fire Department. I will drop anything and everything to go help when someone calls. Living 8 miles from the Fire Station, if the emergency is in my area I am usually the first responder on the scene, so the quicker I can arrive the more helpful I can be. When hauling logs with the prehauler or up in the woods skidding with the tractor, I try to keep an ATV close in case there is a page for someone in crisis.

My new Honda 420 cc 4X4 is pretty quiet and goes just about anywhere I want here on the farm. I carry tools and trainees - and frequently patrol the forest to keep an eye on everything. A neighbor has had their "mature" trees marked by a consulting forester for harvest. The trees are marked right up to our boundary line. I have taken photos of the area for future reference and patrol the boundary every chance I have so I know when the work is being done.

One of the Oldest Tricks in the Book, in the timber industry, is for a logger to cross a boundary, take the neighbors trees, and if they get caught, say they simply made a mistake. If they do occasionally get caught - they may then have to pay for the trees, stilling earning themselves a good profit.

This just happened again in Southern Wisconsin and it made the papers and TV news. The Sheriff and young reporters naively put out a warning to other landowners, all letting the loggers off the hook for this "simple mistake" because after all, they did pay for the trees once they got caught. The police have more important issues than to worry about a few low value trees now and then. So this goes on and on.

A fellow recently called for help from Arkansas – this happened on his family land this winter. His neighbor was harvesting trees, the loggers crossed the boundary and took all the good trees from this man's property. Law enforcement has been of no help, the forestry appraisal of "market value" is ridiculously low, the forest is gone. Bad situation with no good solution – beware and protect your land!

I keep a close eye on what happens on all our neighbors land, to protect my good trees! My ATV and Trails are essential.

Utility Vehicles

A Husqvarna UTV "side by side" is another part of our fleet. Here Jack is skidding a birch log with the ATV Arch and is carrying firewood from the tree tops. Simply being able to carry home the firewood or Shiitake logs when clearing fallen branches or trees from the trail system makes this machine valuable. Always carry a chain saw and do some collecting while in the woods to take advantage of all the opportunities out there.

Golf Cart

Tracy's old golf cart is now another machine to get people up through the woods. Simple, fast, quiet, versatile. With good tires, this easy to climb into cart - simple to operate, is perfect for the older generations that have more difficulty with trails and hills.

Logging Arches

Mark Havel, our friend & owner of Future Forest Products in Oregon, revitalized the use of logging arches 20 years ago. Arches are nothing new – one of the traditional tools used to tame the wilderness and clear cut the original American forests.

Lifting most of the weight of the log off of the ground, and carrying it on two wheels, reduces the power needed by about half.

The log is kept cleaner and the ground is not ripped up and rutted.

ATV Arch is fast and fun – for small scattered trees what need to be hauled in good weather.

A Fetching Arch and Winch with Radio Control are an awesome team that empowers me to skid large oak trees up the hills through the forest to our trails.

Arches and Winches can be used to move big logs in yards around homes. Carrying the heavy log on wheels protects a yard from skidding damage and lessens the power needed, also.

Forwarding Trailers

Many sizes of log hauling trailers are available for urban, plantation, and natural forestry. These are very practical and useful in many situations. Again, using small equipment is practical and profitable if you sell high value products from our efforts. Our forwarder is kept on the trails in the woods, we don't drive around through the natural forest with any machines - so we don't damage the regeneration and soils.

A log loader lifts the logs into the bed, so the full weight of the logs are carried on 4 or more wheels. The loader is powered by the tractor hydraulic pump, or can have its' own gas engine and pump. A steerable draw bar (the Majaco trailer has a hydraulic steering option) makes the trailer more maneuverable on a curvy woods trail.

There are many tricks to loading large logs with small equipment. On my trip to Germany in 2004, one stop to watch a trucker load 20 meter long logs with a short loader – showed me tricks I had never seen watching American truckers moving short logs with long loaders for decades. Watch and learn and adapt is the path to profit!

A winch is really nice to be able to skid logs close enough to grab with the loader. I also carry a long nylon strap that can be used to extend the reach of my loader.

This trailer is great that it can be used in the woods and on the roads. In our business, the machines that do double or triple duty are the most rewarding to own.

Flat Bed Trailers –

We have a flat bed trailer for moving logs on the road. The old fashioned way of rolling logs onto a load still works –

Summary – Moving Logs

We only move logs when the ground is firm – we never damage our soil and trails. If the trails are wet we can work inside the barn and make flooring or run the sawmill under the roof.

Ground skidding with a winch or horse – takes lots of power, gets the log thoroughly dirty all around, while likely doing damage to the ground and the trail.

Arch Skidding – uses about half the power needed to drag a log on the ground, you carry most of the weight on wheels, this keeps the log clean on 3 sides, you can move much faster & quieter.

Forwarder and Trailer – carrying the logs on 4 tires requires 25% of the power needed to ground skid, keeps the logs clean all around. Hauling uphill is even practical, roads are protected with firm ground.

Trying to make the biggest haul at one time usually leads to disaster, damage, and wasted time. I go for overall efficiency, often taking a few quick smaller loads rather than maxing out the equipment with too heavy a load of logs.

Use The Best Tool for every job – all of these are best seen to believe.

Sawmilling logs to make high value products

Most sawmills have gone out of business the last few decades – globalization has taken the profit from this step in the commodity market in the USA. Low labor costs and few regulations on business plus government subsidies along the way - give the sawmills on the other side of the world the major advantage to make stuff cheaply. People here have mostly chosen cheap imported stuff on sale. Now most of the wood products in our stores are imported from another country, while our local trees are neglected, undervalued, and mismanaged – and our State's businesses wilt away.

While most other sawmills failed, our Timbergreen Farm sawmill has become more profitable every year as we make higher and higher value products from our trees and sell direct to our customers. You simply have to plan to make money – know your products in advance and sell direct to customers. There is plenty of value in wood products if you learn to earn them.

We use a small band sawmill for most of our logs – a WoodMizer. The inexpensive blade of a WoodMizer is the basis for the new revolution in using street trees and yard trees that likely have overgrown metal inside. Large sawmills won't risk damage to their expensive blades, but my WoodMizer bandsaw blade is $25 – the value of one average board that I saw. Hitting metal is no longer a discouragement to using urban trees – this changes everything in Urban tree use!

How Do They Do It – measuring and valuing wood

In the timber business, we estimate the volume and value of wood many different ways as it progresses through the system from standing tree to finished product. Lots of opportunities for "fuzzy math".

A selected, marked standing tree is measured and the volume & value estimated, so a lump sum price can be agreed upon in advance for a planned and marked timber harvest. The volume estimate table uses the trees outer circumference measurement at 4 ½ feet off the ground - or the Diameter Breast Height, plus the height as estimated by number of 16 foot logs that will likely be made once the tree is felled. This method may work with telephone pole shaped Douglas Fir, but hardwoods have a different shape, lots of taper, large branches and various defects. Long story made short – the tree volume estimate scale used by foresters when marking timber for a lump sum sale, underestimates the actual volume of hardwood trees by about 25%.

The growers usually don't know this – they trust the professional forester to represent their interest and be ethical. The buyers know this and adjust their bids on many factors. In theory it all averages out in the end – but in a one sided market, as usual the timber grower and local community get the short end of the stick.

Once the trees are felled and bucked into logs, each piece is again measured to determine the diameter of each log at the small end, inside the bark. Deductions are made for defects and deviations from straight. In most lump sum timber sales, with a payment made in advance to avoid questions later, the logger produces 25% more volume than the forester's standing tree estimate. In a perfect world this all averages out in the market, but in reality the logger and buyer usually skim the icing off the cake here without the landowner knowing the full story.

Those of us modern sawmillers who use a WoodMizer or other small bandsaw mill with a thin kerf blade, gain another 25% in lumber over the volume estimate of the log volume previously measured. The old tables were based on big thick circular sawmills that made a lot of sawdust with every cut. A thin sawmill blade yields another serving of icing that is available to the savy sawyer, and likely is unknown or understood by the tree's grower.

Knowing the final product that you will make also allows the smart sawmiller to cut the exact size pieces needed, likely yielding more usable boards per sawn log for the businessman in complete control. For our flooring and most other products, I always save an extra 6% on each board in thickness, because I know I can. Then I save another 10%, then another 10%, then more…. Because I know I can.

A pile of lumber will shrink back about 25% when flooring or other products are made due to straightening, trimming, cutting out bad defects and making the Tongue & Groove. We have lots of tricks to save here and make money there all along the way, because we know we can.

Installing the character grade mixed species flooring we make allows us to use most of the tree and earn retail prices for our salvaged trees that far exceeds the understanding and experience of all the "experts" who just talk and write about forestry stuff. Bottom line, if you are not earning thousands of dollars per tree and thousands of dollars per acre per year for your forest growth, read on.

The final sales bring the real results – all the hype in the middle is noise and mystery. Here are the real results of what we do here with commercially worthless trees while we let our good trees just keep on growing.

Examples of earning the Full Value of a Tree

	Small tree 10"	Average tree 18"	Good tree 30"
Tree scale volume estimate	not even on scale	200 bf	600 bf
value of tree standing	20 cents	$40	$240
Log scale (diameter/length)	10 bf	250 bf	750bf
value of logs at sawmill	$2	$100	$500
Lumber scale	25 bf	310 bf	950 bf
value of lumber	$20	$400	$2,500
Flooring Strips	20 sqft	250 sqft	750 sqft
value of flooring strips	$60	$750	$3,500
Installed Flooring	$200	$2,500+	$9,500++

install matching baseboard – add 10% to the total flooring job

Getting to the value of the flooring strips is most of the work, and the most difficult part of the whole job. Installing and finishing the flooring can triple your income with just a little more work – is the safest & easiest part of the whole job, and builds your business in many ways. This creates complete control and understanding and knowledge of your product – priceless!

Mixed species flooring is the best opportunity of all to use the natural output of a forest area. Most of the tree can be made into flooring or even higher value products. We can earn $10 per board foot or better for most trees with flooring, but much higher prices per board foot are earned with many other products. Build a foundation with flooring, then expand to the sky with other solid wood products.

Do Just the Opposite

The myths taught to me by the "experts" of "juvenile box wood", pallet lumber and railroad ties was quickly exposed to the realities of owning forest land. I sold pallet lumber and cants (at a loss) one time, never again. I realized our trees never went to college.

I sold "graded" lumber one time. Sawmilling for grade lumber – the American Way - is extremely complicated and technical. Sawing for grade, you are competing with the biggest most modern & computerized sawmills of all. Grade sawing is sawmilling from the outside towards the center, continuously rotating the log and taking the best board with clear cuttings of wood. I don't try to compete with the big sawmills anymore. I work a smarter and simpler system of value, not volume.

I have three methods that I use to saw most logs.

The Timbergreen Techniques

Live Sawmilling

The most frequent method is also the oldest method – live sawmilling, flitch sawing, sawing through and through. This is the European method still used on many logs in the mills I visited in Germany. Gang sawing makes all the boards in one pass through the powerful machine in a big factory. Precise and simple and fast

I position the log on the WoodMizer and saw a few flitches, then rotate the log one time. Then I simply saw down to the bed, making many boards with minimal work. This saws with the wood grain most of the time.

We use this method nearly all the time with small diameter and curved logs and character logs. We do this on the WoodMizer and the resaw. Most logs can be sawmilled with this method. Anyone can sawmill a good log – it takes some thought to process the majority of logs and earn a good profit.

Number Two

Simple Sawmilling

Square up and saw down is what I do with knotty logs and dirty logs. Simple, fast – take a slab & one board, rotate 90 degrees, take a slab and one board – rotate 90 degrees, take a slab and one board, rotate the final quarter turn. Take the slab and saw right on down the cant to the bed of the sawmill.

I dry my lumber, then do the sorting and manufacturing to get the highest value product from each piece of the tree. So we really do need to think carefully and make good decisions at this stage, but this is the best time of all to do that when you really know what you have to work with. Stress and cracks show most clearly once the boards come out of the kiln. I would rather the stresses show early than late when processing boards, so you can simply work around them to make the best final products.

Foresters and woodworkers are supposed to be really really really smart = as they are always predicting the future and playing God – knowing what will happen over the next hundred years or so for each important decision made. I got tired of trying to figure all that out, and messing up every time anyway – and just simplified things to where I don't have to think so much anymore. Now I know a simple process to earn thousands of dollars per tree and will stick with that unless I would find something better.

The Third – and most challenging & rewarding
3. Quartersawmilling

The good straight logs are mostly quartersawn, to get that specific grain pattern in our boards. This is an old method that dates back to before there were lumber dry kilns. Quartersawn or vertical grain boards are more stable and shrink less in width than flat sawn boards. The look of the ray flecks in the quartersawn grain of Oak has a traditional pattern many people like. Cherry, Maple, Elm, Hackberry, Walnut, Ash, Honey Locust... and many others have spectacular fine ray flecks that give these boards a special look (especially in the sunlight!) farther South, many more species had exemplary quarter sawn grain patterns well worth exposing and featuring!!

I have many videos and written features on the details of quartersawmilling logs on the WoodMizer, so I won't repeat these lessons here – simply do a little googling if you want to learn about this. Really, This is a whole other book of details to explore and release and showcase the wonderful wood grain of logs of all species of trees – for spectacular finished products of highest value possible for people to appreciate and love for a lifetime.

Thrills unlimited!

Timber felling and quartersawmilling and installing and selling - are the most challenging, interesting, rewarding, and exciting things about Good Local Wood that make my life unique and worth living today. Everything else is pretty good and OK too, but the highlights are worth focusing on.

Volume vs Value

Since I make high value products from my trees, I'm not in a big hurry to produce large volumes of wood to sell at commodity prices. When you earn thousands of dollars per tree, you can take your time to do things right – so you can feel good about what you are doing and what you are leaving for the future.

A commercial logger has a number of trees per day, a volume of cords to produce, to break even, pay the monthly bills, and hope to make a profit. I just do what is good for my forest and know that the value of the wood products I am making - justifies my efforts and time and investments.

Sawmilling

Sawmilling is a lot of hard work and is kind of dirty sometimes too. Knowing what products will be made, doing the woodworking, selling the products to customers and seeing the finished products installed in the customer's home - makes all the hard work very rewarding both spiritually and financially.

Resaws Reign for small diameter logs

Most sawmills have a resaw to do repetitive cuts on cants made by the headsaw. The log is made into large pieces that have pre-planned boards inside. The resaw makes the routine final cuts, freeing the more expensive and powerful headsaw to break down more logs. Initially, the cants from the outside of the log contain higher value lumber, then the center cant – the middle of the log - is sent to another resaw to be made into pallet parts.

We have adapted the simple resaw – used to make the most basic, low value pallet pieces – to perform three very important processes for our business.

    We use our resaw to sawmill small diameter logs into high value boards
    We use our resaw to make curved cants into uniform thickness lumber while quartersawing
    We use our resaw to make thin laser stock boards from thick dry lumber.

A simple resaw holds the magic to make plantation forestry and all of forestry profitable by making small diameter logs into high potential value lumber. Cheap, accurate, efficient, simple, productive… Marketing the wood for high value products is the key – pallets are the lowest value use, but the same wood can be worth 100 times more with some smarts and marketing.

I can train a pair of workers to operate a resaw in a few hours – for primary production first, then maybe a little simple secondary work too. This inexpensive sawmill is very efficient and makes consistently uniform thickness lumber.

Chain Saw Sawmilling

Large logs exceed my ability to move or sawmill the huge heavy pieces, so the Chain Saw Sawmill extends our ability to process big trees into high value products. We only use this tool as the last option as it is noisy and wasteful and slow. But sometimes – this is the key to success.

The good news is this machine is cheap and portable.   A complete tool chest is very rewarding in all of forest management!!

More and more we use this as the first step in processing, just to break down a log into manageable and moveable pieces, then get down to details back at the kiln and shop.

Slabwood tables….

One slab table per year on the average is all I can boast over 4 decades. We can make a lot more money resawing and making higher value stuff from thick slabs, but these real wood works of art are special and add to the portfolio of products we can offer to wood lovers all over. I love the natural look of a huge hunk of timber, so we keep this option on the table for our customers, but we would likely starve on this single idea as a business model.

Our current business model uses the Chain saw sawmill – the Alaskan Mill to slab up a huge tree so we can move and dry the manageable slab pieces. When dry, we resaw the big chunks into smaller more saleable and profitable products.

The Peterson, Swing Saw, sawmill and planer

This is one machine I have not owned, so take this with what it is worth…. Everything else here is stuff I have done and worked out and tested and know and can do before I write or speak. But I have seen this tool in action around the world and have been amazed. A unique machine with special uses that are the best fit many times. Check it out.

Selling to Customers

"This wood is way more beautiful than I ever expected!" We get the Best feedback ever from our customers and retail prices over and over. We just booked the 11th floor installation for a family near here. Repeat business is the best!

Timber Growers and local communities and professional sawyers all need to experience this reward! Not knowing where your wood goes to, just feeding the supply chain, makes the work just work. We see our efforts come to fruition – it is a wonderful thing to know how a tree ends up in someone's home as a useful and beautiful product.

If you have settled for less – wake up and grab a new opportunity to live!

This would change the world if people understood how our resources were used – we would value our trees and land in a new way, a better way.

Everyone but a very few rich folk would welcome this change.

Too bad just a few rich folk run our world and the rest of us allow it to happen and make it happen with our purchasing choices.

The internet tools and global travel can bring things back into balance.

Chapter Nine Trapping Free Solar Power to dry wood

Trees and plants are the most efficient solar energy collecting and storage devices. Photosynthesis goes on even on a cloudy day, making plant material that can be used for food and fuel when we want it. I see this when I burn wood in my stove to heat my log home – I see the sunlight being released and feel the sun's heat again when I need it.

The sun's energy can be felt on your skin and everyone has experienced the extreme heat that quickly builds up in a closed automobile when the sun shines in. Multiply that by 100 times and you start to get the idea of a solar heated kiln to dry lumber.

We use natural and efficient solar energy to heat air to dry our lumber. The natural daily cycle of sunshine and darkness actually works to our advantage in drying wood, producing a superior quality lumber compared to a commercial kiln schedule that heats the wood continuously to produce the maximum volume of dry boards. Other uses of solar energy struggle with storing the power for use at other times, we simply use it all right when the sun shines.

Kiln Unloading Day is Amazing

The time spent taking the lumber out of the kiln is quite emotional. This is where you really get to see the potential values of the finished wood products that are now possible. Producing high quality lumber from worthless trees and drying them with free solar power, putting local people to work – is all very exciting and rewarding to me.

Occasionally there is disappointment when the boards are too warped or split up, and we work to learn to do better next time. My timber felling skills and log bucking methods and sawmilling techniques are all much higher as a result of the direct feedback I get every time I help unload a kiln.

There are many types of kilns that can be used to dry lumber. Traditionally, wood waste was burned to generate the heat that is needed, now natural gas is easier. One reason I prefer to use free solar power is that I can avoid using fossil fuels that add carbon to the atmosphere while adding to the huge profits of the big energy corporations.

The Three Key types of wood used for success by small local business can be dried effectively in Solar Cycle Kilns. The nightly equalization cycle lets these kilns carefully dries these types of lumber that are considered not practical in commercial dry kilns. Being able to produce high value wood products from commercially worthless trees is a major factor in promoting Good Local Wood.

> Small diameter logs and the centers of larger logs, are said by the experts - to contain "juvenile box wood" that is too reactive to dry for high value products. This huge quantity of wood has traditionally only been used for low value products like railroad ties, mine timbers, pallet parts, and wood boxes. Solar Cycle Kilns successfully dry the wood grain from young fast growing trees for use in high value products like flooring, cutting boards, plaques, countertops, etc...

The mix of species dries well in a Solar Cycle Kiln, as all of the boards equalize in moisture content at night and on cloudy days.

> Curved boards with bark and lumber only half usable can be dried efficiently in a Solar Cycle Kiln because the heat source is free. Gaining high value products from worthless wood makes the extra handling and effort all worth while to a small business in the local economy.

The Four Parts of a Solar Cycle Lumber Kiln

Insulated wood room – keep the heat you collect when the sun shines
Clear window facing the sun – keep out the rain, let in the sun
Black metal collecting surface – recycled corrugated roofing is best
Small electric fan to circulate the air – just enough to move the hot air

Our kilns work on the principle of using free wind energy to completely pre-dry the lumber for free before putting the lumber into the solar heated kiln cycle. Minimizing the amount of moisture in the Solar Cycle Kiln keeps it very simple and inexpensive compared to a commercial kiln that produces large volumes of water vapor and lumber.

New Solar Cycle Kiln under construction

My three Solar Cycle Kilns here at Timbergreen Farm are 28, 25 and 21 years old. The planned life use for each kiln was 15 years. Each now has its own personality and problems, but they still dry more wood that we can use. The first one costs about a penny per board foot for the electricity needed to power the fans to circulate the hot air. Now, modern versions are ten times more efficient with an electricity cost of one tenth of a cent per board foot.

One new kiln could outdo all three old ones, but they still work and dry our wood.

Maintenance is steady – every day or every opportunity, I listen to my kilns – even from 200 yards away on my home's deck, and I know from the sound if things are good or need service in one of the kilns. I know my forest and my machines. I can hear and feel and sense the condition of each facet of my business. "Be One With The Machine" – Sense the Spirit of the Forest – if you can spend the time to learn this intimacy with your equipment and source - your level of satisfaction with your work is greatly magnified. Lucky for me my Dad is a professional Electrical Engineer, retired – available and free to do the needed motor repair when needed. I have all my workers and friends drop off their broken appliances and motors to try and keep him occupied in his leisure years on the farm. We have a wonderful multi-generational family based business going here, fueled by the value of the naturally dying trees in our forests.

Russian Kiln Now I get it

Sergei, a wildlife park manager in Eastern Russia with 10,000 acres of forest – and a woodworker - had read our materials, viewed the blueprints, and seen the pictures of our kilns. He came to the USA and visited Timbergreen Farm with a group of mostly other Sergei's from what I could understand. Sergei #1 immediately disappeared from the tour group – last seen headed up the hill towards the kilns. 20 minutes later he reappeared and exclaimed in enthusiastic robust Russian – "Now I Get It!"

I know the feeling – the first time I walked into Scott Stoke's super-sized solar kilns in Mazomanie Wi in 1984, it was a life changing experience - to feel the awesome power of the sunlight being put to a really good use. The annoying heat that builds up in a closed car on a sunny day is multiplied by a hundred times, added to by tropical humidity way more impressive than any

rainforest jungle, and it is all working to do important work on our lumber that doubles the value of the board, for about free.

You have to feel this to believe it – we offer tours!

Michigan Kiln - North South – two sided roof collector polycarbonate

Tennessee Kiln

Greene Kiln

New Zealand Kiln use the extra heat to add to different rooms

Simple Solar Cycle Kiln – likely best idea of all for the people of the planet but too simple to believe

Everything as of 2014 is printed in my book Solar Cycle Lumber Kilns. Here is what is new for 2105….

New rooftop collector kiln

We recently bought a 3,500 sqft pole and truss structure building to house our laser shop and retail store, on State Highway 23 in Spring Green – the route travelled by everyone visiting Taliesin, House on the Rock, American Players Theatre along with Mineral Point and Wisconsin Dells, among many other destinations.

The metal rooftop everyday reflects away several hundred dollars worth of free solar energy. In our region, every square meter of land is bombarded with about six kilowatt hours of energy every day. Another example of Use it or Lose it.

Phase one is to attach a solar cycle collector the same size as each of our collectors here at Timbergreen – 40 feet long by 15 feet tall = facing the sun at a 45 degree angle, our latitude. An outside insulated wood room on the ground will be used to dry 1,000 board feet of lumber every month.

The costs for the materials are about $5,000 and we will catch about $100 per day in free energy. The value gained from the kiln drying process will be about $12,000 per year. When we also figure in the middlemen profit we keep by selling finished products, our benefits are doubled again at this step.

Clear roofing for our big window

Most greenhouse materials and roofing is made to reflect away the heat of the sun. Too much heat is normally the more aggravating problem so window materials are coated and insulated to keep the heat out, even in climates where we buy a lot of heat energy. We found that clear tarps and roofing from Canada are clearer and less likely to reflect the heat. Be sure your material is as clear as possible.

One layer window

Our first kilns had two layers of plastic that was inflated into an insulated window. We learned that indeed the insulated window did conserve the collected solar heat, but also the two layers of poly tarp reflected heat away also. Two layers is more expensive and involves another small fan to keep the space between the layers inflated. I have no definitive conclusion today as to which is better – no major difference – so my choice is simple is best.

My choice for the new collector on the roof is one clear corrugated solid sheet of polycarbonate roofing. The initial cost is higher but the strength of the clear panels and a longer useful life are the important factors on this one.

Barn fan

Since our new building is in the village with neighbors on each side, a slower speed larger diameter Barn Fan will circulate the air in this kiln with less noise. The fan will only run during direct sunshine, and the noise of the State Highway is way more noticeable, but minimizing the affect on our neighbors can only be a good thing. A variable speed control will move more air when the sun is the brightest.

Since we pre dry our lumber completely to 10-12% Moisture Content, there is little moisture left in the wood we place in the insulated kiln chambers. It is the heat doing the work in removing the final moisture from the boards, the air flow only needs to circulate the air slowly, compared to the initial phase of fresh-sawn wet lumber drying, where surface evaporation is the main action. Wet your finger and blow on it to feel this effect of wind velocity on drying a moist surface.

Phase two will utilize the entire South facing roof surface – 100 feet long by 15 feet tall.

Just multiply the area of your roof and parking lots… by 6 kilowatt hours every day that is not being used, maybe even just overheating your environment so **you need to buy more energy to cool off** again.

Use it or Lose it is so true with Solar energy.

Using the south facing wall of the building is another way to use simple solar methods to catch the heat of the sun on good days. Vertical surfaces catch the most energy in the winter when the angle of the sun is lower and more direct on vertical walls. Reflection of the sun's heat from the ground onto a vertical wall is greatest with snow on the ground, when we can use the heat the most!

As this is a work in progress – up to the minute information can be accessed at www.TimbergreenFarm.com

The Book - Solar Cycle Lumber Kilns (2014) by Jim Birkemeier shares 26 years of information on the design, building, and operating success of this system. The website has the info to obtain this book.

Chapter Ten Make High-Value Stuff

Cutting down a living tree is a sad experience for most humans – it is a killing.

The people of Spring Green were quite upset by the actual taking of these street trees to widen Jefferson St even after years of planning.   When they saw our business was going to be able to use the wood, much of the emotional responses were lessened. Most people feel that it is much worse to kill a tree if the wood is wasted.

Salvaging a dead tree is very different – it is a saving, a preserving, an honoring, a rescue……

Many of us feel a spiritual connection to living trees – different from human contact but something real and significant in a quieter realm. I Sense the spirit of every forest I encounter – and every tree that I come close too. Tree hugging is amazing – more basic than just hugging other person. I find that hugging a tree is a certain knowing = while squeezing a human may be a mushy questionable thing. There is not anything sexual in hugging a tree – it is just sensing the strength and life of the tree = the want to live and prosper and grow and make a difference for making all this fuss here.   Trees want to live beyond their life in the sun = we can cooperate together to forge projects to live together into the future.

Honoring a Tree's Life with a lasting product lessens the sadness we feel.

Releasing the trees spirit in a work of art for others to enjoy is the best. A local artist Bill Wilkie shows off the spirit of wood in his art!! Seeing the vision and cutting away the waste to reveal the work of art.

Honor the tree's work – preserve the wood for the future – don't waste it

Bring a Dead Tree Back To Life in a Useful product for the future.

The last tree I salvaged - the dead White Oak up on the ridge top – was 150 years old. 2 1/2 times my age = my great great great grandpa was alive = The Civil War was raging, Lincoln was President in office…. Our farm was being settled and farmed for the first time ever.   History, the story in the stump is right there for you to see and appreciate and understand and learn from.

Cattle grazed here for a century. We saw in the growth rings a ground fire burned through this ridge top in 1923.   The last harvest in 1963 was barely evident in this tree but obvious in other trees we counted over the other salvages up here on this ridge over the last 30 years.   You learn about your forest by reading the tree rings as you work!

Most other forest owners or home owners have no idea what happens to their trees once the truck hauls away the logs from their property. People don't connect the high value of finished wood products back to the potential opportunities in the trees growing all around. City folk don't understand that the wood products they buy are made from trees just like the ones growing all around them.

Wood products are one material that is simple and practical to manufacture and sell on a small scale in the local community. Wood working is a traditional way of life now quickly being lost to industrialization. Skills can be easily learned for making the vast majority of wood products.

Good Use of Machines

We use simple tools to make high value products. Our workshop operation is quite basic; table saw, chop saw, planer, jointer, shaper, band saw, drill press, sanders, lathe. With these tools we can make just about anything with wood.

We always try to make new things with these old tools to earn success.

The best example is we use our band resaw at the sawmill to make the highest value products of all in our line. The resaw is about the simplest machine used in the sawmill industry, primarily to make the lowest value product of all – pallet pieces from fresh sawn lumber. I made pallet lumber one time and realized that is not going to work around here.

Our edger saw at the sawmill building is a second basic machine the industry uses for simple work to remove bark from sawn lumber, while we use our edger as a rip saw to make high value products from kiln dry lumber. We leave the bark on the boards into the kiln to use much of it in unique natural products or dry fuel.

The value we create making and selling high value finished products is virtually limitless and mind boggling. No forester anywhere can even begin to relate to the high values of products we sell from our salvaged trees. We do offer tours here all the time as this stuff really needs to be seen in person to be appreciated and believed.

I repeatedly use the value of $10 per board foot or Ten Thousand dollars per Thousand board feet as the break even point for our business, or the level of income that makes us a profit. We can take just about any tree to this level, but this is really just where we start today to earn more and more from our trees each year. If you want the real secrets we use today, you will have to visit here and try to steal them for yourself – I can't give away everything.

"If you want perfect – buy plastic!"

We make wood products that are unique and as natural as possible, with lots of hands-on work. I don't try to compete with a huge factory full of big machines. As every tree is unique, every piece of wood is one of a kind. I work with that and show it off, not try to make it look perfect like plastic. My fingerprints are all over my wood products and my customers love it. I sell to people who appreciate real wood and a person that they know.

The perfect wood customer says = price is no object. Using your own wood to build your own home is priceless

Selling Good Local Wood – Telling the whole story

Even when we think about Made in the USA – There is a difference between local small business and big business = choose to support local small VS robots and big machines

Huge Corporations including Rainforest Liquidators make huge profits selling cheap imported products "on sale". They even claim to use wood that is "sustainably harvested" and that all their products are totally good and safe. Most customers apparently want to be fooled that all of these claims are true and that they got a really good deal buying the cheapest stuff ever.

Save money and live better works really well for a few far away corporate executives and distant shareholders, but subjects the masses of people around the world to a downward spiral of economic and environmental and political disasters.

The only remaining commercially profitable product in our region is Basket Ball Court Floors. Our Sports Floor Company has been bought out by foreigners, but at least some of our Wisconsin & Michigan wood still supplies the big business of college sports.

Buying cheap imported stuff on sale in the big corporation's store, or online, is what kills our economy - we are choosing this ourselves.

When you buy cheap stuff on sale from a big corporation...

You are totally supporting the cheapest possible labor working in the worst possible conditions

You are absolutely supporting jobs on the other side of the world

You are obviously supporting the lowest satisfaction jobs on all sides of the world

You are discouraging the small locally owned businesses in your community

You are foolishly supporting the maximum energy use in production and transportation

You are willingly supporting the most environmental abuse of the resources

You are flagrantly supporting the most damaging practices of pollution and biggest eco-disasters

You are blindly supporting the most influential political power brokers

And when something is on a really big hyped up sale....

You are probably buying defective, inferior, unwanted, and otherwise unsellable stuff.

You are supporting the minimum wage job opportunities in your local community

And people believe it when they say you will live better??

Made in the USA   Grown & Made in Wisconsin Dane Buy Local   Wisconsin Urban Wood

The time is right to build a new brand of Good Local Wood – right now!

Together, we all choose to create local jobs or send them overseas. We choose to undercut or build our local companies.

It is what we choose to buy that controls the global economy today - every single purchase you choose is a real and immediate vote for the future.

What we buy everyday controls everything on the planet, including our economy, our environment, our politicians and our military.

We are in a new global economy and society - we need to choose the good opportunities and avoid the problems. The good should win if we are wise.

We need to buy the best value - a combination of price we pay and the costs and benefits to the planet.

We need to see the big picture and the impact of each product we buy. Put our creative energy into this and we can change the world.

In general, the trends of big corporations dominating the planet's resources are bad - these monsters are wreaking havoc on humanity and our natural resource. All we have to do is stop feeding the monsters and they will quickly fade away.

Choose to buy as local as possible from as small a business as possible

choose as hand made as possible   the best value for the future

choose the most natural wood product possible

and we will find the best balance possible for our future

If we would all share in the value of wood products - then everyone else = the vast majority of the people on this planet will benefit from our trees efforts. There are still plenty of trees and unlimited solar energy coming into our planet every day for our use to live together throughout the future.

Chapter Eleven Sell High-Value Stuff

The most rewarding thing to do with your own trees is to use the wood to build yourself a beautiful home. Gordon Greene built this spectacular timber frame home just South of Spring Green using the wood from his land. Once you finish your home, selling your extra wood to customers in your own community is very rewarding also.

A floor board can be made from a tree from our forest, from a tree grown along the side of a village street, from a neighbor's back yard, a fencerow tree, a tree from a park…. Wood products can come from about any tree and most any tree can be used to make high value beautiful wood products. Most trees have the potential to be used for a lasting piece of wood furniture or ….. any of a thousands things. Not every tree is good enough to use, but there are Billions of local trees - undervalued and underutilized in the traditional timber markets - that could make valuable products and put local people to work. Some basic information can help sort all this out to earn the values of Good Local Wood.

Wood products are one material that is simple and practical to manufacture and sell on a small scale in the local community. And trees grow more every year – the supply is huge and expanding.

Here at Timbergreen Farm, we sell our wood every way possible. People stop by the sawmill wanting to buy boards, we install floors in a customer's home & they show their new floor to friends & family – selling more of our floors, people come in our retail store to buy wood, online shoppers order our products from a wide variety of websites, we ship quantities of wholesale products to other stores that we made contact with at trade shows, and we sell products on the street at the Arts & Crafts Fair plus the Farmer's Markets.

You have to make things that people want to buy – what Women want

You have to be unique and lead the way = sell art and not crafts. Be creative and hand made

Be Searchable – one of a kind - express yourself

Sell your story, your self and your wood.

Personalize the piece for the customer and you can double the value.

Packaging/labeling makes your product stand out and be recognized.

Be real, stress natural, promote hand made, keep it solid – stand out in the crowd of cheap manufactured products that flood the marketplace. Sell a unique work of real hand made art that is priceless and success can be yours!

I just bought some bearings for a glider rocker project. Prices vary all over for the same thing and I worked hard to find the cheapest deal to maximize my profit when I sell the wood rocker from some Good Urban Wood. When buying a commodity, cheap is good – but you don't want to sell a commodity.

Making wood is Easy - Selling Wood is Hard Work

Selling is work, but nothing new. You can learn to sell wood – the variety of products and sales methods are unlimited. Copy what works for other people, just do it a little different and a little better and smarter.

Use the media with your unique story. Most of my progress the past 4 decades came with free stories in the printed media.   But the results are not always immediately good. Many people say Any Publicity is Good Publicity, even if it looks bad at first.

Even good PR can cause problems though. When getting noticed backfires – use it to your advantage

Sauk County Zoning hassled our small WoodMizer sawmill for years, considering it the same way as a large commercial sawmill, needing expensive permits and their out of date approvals, costing thousands of dollars. We stood up to the old stupid laws and got TV and front page stories. It was likely our family's best publicity ever in the local area. I got a lot more "thank you"s and pats on the back and "way to go's and respect for standing up to the zoning administrators than all the years I have stood up for the forest.

Buying and selling local wood is a community effort – the two are totally connected.

Everywhere that I have been – the limiting factor on a woodworking business is the number of customers who buy good local wood. It is easy to make boards and wood products, but selling to the customer is the key. If more people buy my wood products, the more people I can hire and keep busy, and the more values that will come from our local trees.

Leaders and educators need to encourage everyone to use good local wood. Small business can not compete with the big global corporate advertisers – the community has to learn the values of using good local wood.

Forest owners have been so beaten down on timber prices by the timber industry and forestry profession that most can't believe their trees have significant value. Forest owners have no idea what happens to their trees once the truck hauls away the logs. Most of the wood products in our stores today are imported from another country. Bad trends getting worse every day

We can look around and see trees all over, in our yards, along the streets, in the forests. When we look in the store for wood products, most if it is imported from other countries. Our local trees are not being used. We choose to by cheap imports and let our local wood go to waste. Buying cheap stuff on sale comes at a very high cost to our planet.

The whole community can work together to make and sell and buy good local wood. The whole system needs to work together. Our teachers and leaders must understand the basics and support this option for using Good Local Wood.

Someone calls me every day and wants me to buy their trees, logs, lumber that they have extra.

Someone else calls me once in a while and wants to buy a specific wood piece for a project. Rarely do they ask for something that I have available in stock – the variety needed to meet local demand is huge, discouraging small local business and fostering the big box store selling cheap imports of all kinds.

This disconnect between our local forests and local wood needs is frustrating and concerning. The time delays in growing trees, harvesting logs, sawmilling, and drying make buying decisions a matter of timing on someone's part – usually not the buyers planning ahead.

For ten years I just sold dry lumber to other woodworkers. This is an OK business – there are plenty of trees around and sawmilling & drying is simple. If you salvage local wood, sawmill & dry efficiently, there is enough value in the boards to operate a business on a limited scale. The drawback to just selling lumber is that most people want just good boards and a tree makes both good boards and a lot of other boards that aren't all that good to sell. People like to sort through the supply and pick just the ones they want, often leaving a mess. Most boards are sellable to someone as long as you encourage the type of customers who appreciate natural local wood. You need a large inventory of species, thickness, lengths, grades, and moisture content to satisfy the most customers possible. Your store needs to be open most hours of the week to be available to the variety of customers. A planer and rip saw offer services in high demand when selling boards.

The older I get, with limited energy and ambition, the more I want to sell finished products at higher values per board foot. We learned to use most all of the reject lumber from our first decade of selling, to make character grade flooring, but it is a lot more fun to use the good boards yourself. Manufacturing and selling high value products is a lot more rewarding and gives me a greater flexibility in my schedule of work and play.

In the trillion dollar per year timber industry, there is room for anyone and everyone to find their most rewarding use of wood. The more people who work with Good Local Wood the better. There is no risk of too many competitors – strength in numbers is the key to changing an old traditional industrial market. Fear and ignorance blocks most change and progress.

This is a win win win situation for almost everyone except the few very rich people who get the Billions in profit from taking advantage of the earth's people and natural resources. Some have used globalization to gain dominance in the timber industry. Local people can now choose to use the good tools of globalization to gain a portion of control in their local communities. Knowing that using Good Local Wood is a workable option is the first step.

One of the most important things about using good local wood is that it directly lowers the demand to clear cut the remaining tropical rainforests, and helps protect all natural forests from illegal logging.

Once in a while there is talk of enforcing existing laws about illegal logging and product safety, and some talk about trade agreements between countries to even the playing field for US companies... If customers chose wisely when purchasing wood products, all this would take care of itself very quickly. When we buy products, that is an instant direct vote of the future. The only power greater than the rich corporations is the buying actions of the American woman – the shoppers are the true real power on the planet. The corporations people buy from the most control the world – it is our choice and chance to control them - with our purchases.

Everyone complains and talks about the economy and jobs and the environment. This simple choice to use local wood keeps our money in the local economy, builds local jobs, and protects & improves our local and global environment in many ways.

Selling to Customers

I make a wood product for my own home first. I practice and learn all about each item and then have a place to show it off too. There are lots of opportunities to donate wood products to public places to get your wood out into view. Just a little confidence is what is needed to sell good wood.

Each new home becomes another showroom and every customer becomes a salesperson. "This is way more beautiful than I ever expected!" We get the Best feedback ever and retail prices over and over.

Timber Growers everywhere, and local communities & professional Foresters all need to experience this reward! This would change the world of forest management if the grower was actually rewarded for their time investment and effort.

Everyone but a very few rich folk would welcome this change.

Too bad just a few rich folk run our world and we allow it to happen. Women – the shoppers – are really the most powerful force on earth. Shopping decisions are what actually run the world – making wise decisions would quickly straighten out most problems today.

Certification as a Sales Tool

Our family farm was Forest Stewardship Council Certified forest and chain of custody business and I was a certified Resource Manager back in 1998, the first in the Lake States Region. We soon found that there indeed was a demand for FSC Certified wood – we got calls from around the world, wanting container loads of top quality lumber of the buyer's choice – at rock bottom prices. We tried to explain that the request is not possible, but not even the foresters working for FSC understood the realities of growing, harvesting, processing and selling wood on a sustainable basis.

Government then big business took over FSC as they have the other certifications. There is insignificant staff to insure any compliance – the certifications are pretty much just bought today, the whole system while sounding good, is pretty much meaningless. All of the talk is uninformed foolishness, people wanting to think they are getting good wood, but they really don't have much of a clue.

Leopold wrote about this all 70 years ago – things really haven't changed much at all. What he saw was needed and it is the same today – the only hope is for wise consumers to choose smart products.

In the global market, there is no way to know. The latest news this week is RainForest Liquidators has relabeled all the poison Chinese flooring to make it sellable to people wanting the cheap stuff.

One way to be confident you are getting good wood is the know your local timber grower.

The internet and global travel can bring things back into balance.
Seeing everything now is gradually ending selfish taking and greed.

Trade Talks and Trips

Our leaders try to control trade and commerce while things and trends continue to slide down hill.

It is crazy for us to sell our very best prime veneer logs to corporations in the Far East, ship the logs half way around the globe, to let them process the wood, and then ship it back to sell the finished product back to us in our local big box stores & online. Buy Local doesn't mean buy cheap imported stuff on sale at your neighborhood big corporation store.

Until sanity in Government is restored, our best action is to buy every single thing with the most wise choice. Research the company we buy from as our purchase supports their political agenda that is way more powerful than our vote on election day.

Silly Stimulus Spending

We need to see that stimulus doesn't work if we go low bid and choose to not support quality and value and local materials and local workers.

If we spend our stimulus money on cheap imported stuff, we do stimulate the economies on the other side of the planet at our own expense.

If we rebuild after a disaster with cheap imported stuff, low bid, illegal labor – everyone loses. FEMA and the Insurance companies are killing our economy by requiring people use stuff as cheap as possible when something bad happens. if we rebuild the community or home with Good Local Wood and local craft workers, a disaster can make things better for the future.

Choose to promote the use of locally grown and manufactured wood products!

We all should focus on supporting our local economy first priority. See and discourage big corporation domination in all its deleterious effects on our planet.

Share and trade when we all benefit. Realize we are all in this together in a limited system. This is the best compromise for all of humanity today

Our global system at the moment is building a few rich people in the big corporations that plunder the earth's resources and take advantage of cheap labor and expend huge amounts of energy shipping stuff to where people buy their cheap stuff. We should be a whole lot smarter.

More than ever before, a few rich people are controlling the new global markets to get way richer, and the masses are falling into lower paying jobs and a poorer environment and despair.

About half of the wood in about half of the local trees around us is suitable for making high value wood products that we can sell to earn a profitable income. That means about ¾ of the volume of local trees needs another market that supports the community also – something that we all need. The mountains of mulch created so far in Urban wood salvage add to the expense of disposing trees, primarily benefiting the wood chipper companies and their friends in government. Why not use this resource to benefit the community?

Trees are likely the best solar energy collectors of all. I heat my home with waste wood. Through the glass door of my wood stove, as wood burns, I see the sunlight being released again and feel the stored heat of the sun radiating out into my house. It is very simple and efficient to burn dry wood. It feels really good to use wood waste and not pay a big energy corporation for their fossil fuel energy. Using carbon energy grown from the sun is way better than burning fossil carbon from underground that puts all that buried carbon up into the atmosphere, contributing to "Global Warming". The exercise in splitting, stacking, and hauling firewood is good for me to.

I heat my hand built log house with my wood scraps, not because I can't pay for propane, but because I can - Not Pay The Big Fuel Companies - and be self-sufficient.

Trees efficiently store the sun's energy in wood, that can be stockpiled and used on demand to provide power for heat and electricity. This energy is renewable and is carbon neutral. The big energy corporations know this and have always blocked significant efforts in the USA to use the energy in wood and other biofuels.   Politics As Usual.

As long as local trees are being cut down anyway, why not use the available energy in the local community? Some wood is currently split up and used for firewood, but the majority is chipped up and wasted at a significant expense to dispose of it. Biofuel is renewable solar energy and we have it – why not use it! If it costs a little more to be energy self-sufficient and carbon neutral, while putting people to work, saving landfill expense….   These trees are already being cut up and chipped and hauled away at a major expense, that could be streamlined into a planned source of biofuel to use renewable energy for all the right reasons. How many oil spills and train wrecks hauling oil do we need to see and how much more global warming documented before we use the renewable fuels right in front of us??

Wood can be burned cleanly as needed to meet local demands. Wood chips – 1" to 2" diameter could be dried with simple solar energy and stored until needed. Wood Gasification is the most efficient and cleanest way to use the energy stored in wood chips. Steam turbines can produce electricity, but having a good local use for the extra heat given off in the process makes the system more efficient. Fine plant materials can be compressed into wood pellets and dried for more efficient burning on a small scale for cooking and heating for personal use.

The power companies won't pay a reasonable or cost effective price for your extra generated electricity so selling it is not a business option. Using the power yourself can make the effort worth while.

Scandinavia is way ahead of us on using biofuels to generate power. All of the methods and machines of all sizes have been perfected and are in use there today.

One suggestion for using all of our local renewable resources is the Good Wood and Food Store

Good Food and Wood and Fuel

Come for a visit at our community's Good Food & Wood & Fuel Store.

When you drive into the parking lot, right away there are many things to see. A grassy area along the road has interesting looking machines and structures with groups of people watching demonstrations. Behind the parking and demonstration yard, there are a variety of solar structures and greenhouses. A retail store boasts a large sign – Good Food & Wood & Fuel. A wide variety of locally grown and manufactured products are sold here. Various other buildings and a pile of logs are seen at the back of the 10 acre facility. It is a unique assemblage of solar collecting buildings that present a flow and purpose.

This facility processes locally grown wood and grows fresh fish and vegetables year around using aquaponics. All the energy needed is produced on the premises from agricultural waste. Neighboring businesses also use electricity generated here, the power lines are leading out from the generating plant. A variety of bio-fuel products are sold in the store. Energy is produced, used, and exported.

Just down the road is a fine family restaurant that sells complete meals of fresh food grown from the facility and neighboring farms. A local brewery and winery sell their products here too. An immense variety of products are available – all from local resources. Every product is sold for its highest value use. Dozens of people have rewarding jobs. Money is kept in the local economy.

Everyone wants to buy local – Here you really can!

This can work in a rural community or on an unused empty lot in a city.
Buying local products keeps our money in the local economy and supports local jobs.

This facility uses the Best of the Best ideas today, in new ways that invigorate local resources. Local forests produce both lumber products and the fuel for heat and electricity to make this business produce fresh food year around. Other agriculture and community waste is also used for energy. The system needs to import some liquid engine fuels, at least for the start up, but the facility produces lots more energy than it uses.

Aquaponics in several greenhouses produce a variety of fresh fish and fresh vegetables all year. By combining these two crops in one closed system, production of both is boosted. To produce fresh food each day, cheap and renewable energy sources are important, especially in an area with cold winters. Solar heating on sunny days is simple using a greenhouse building. During cloudy days and nighttime, two bio-fuel heating and electrical generating systems are used.

The surrounding hillsides have tens of thousands of acres of underutilized forest. Trees are amazing and efficient solar collectors that store the sun's power even on a cloudy day. Wood chips can be dried and stored for use on demand, producing 75% heat and 25% electrical energy. During the winter season, this blend is perfect to provide heat and supplemental lighting for the crops in the aquaponics system. Just waste wood and waste agricultural products are used for fuel

Wood is the perfect fuel for this system

Good logs (and quality grains) are used for higher value uses than energy. Everyone uses wood products – Everyday, Everywhere. Our familiarity with wood products makes it easy for small woodworking ventures to produce useful items and sell them direct to customers close by. While trees and logs are very low value commodities in the industrial timber market, finished wood products are very high value items in the retail market. Capturing that increase in value within the local economy is the brilliance behind this simple system.

The supply of waste wood is huge. Area forests grow several tons of fuel per acre each year. Trees around homes and in communities are continually coming down and are expensive to dispose of. In the city the extra fuel comes more from urban forestry, building renovation, and solid waste.

All the good logs are sawn into lumber and used for high value uses.

Finished wood products are worth 20 to 100 times what a forest owner is paid for standing timber. Wood is easy to work with and can be manufactured into many high value products on a small scale – keeping the value in the local economy. Economic benefits in a local wood business are ten times that of the industrial timber markets. One good local job can be supported for every 40 acres of timber.

Area forest owners learn to manage their timber for many local benefits. Professional timber harvesters use the smallest possible equipment and perform small annual harvests that improve the forest each year. Small truck and trailers haul the logs to the Good Food & Wood & Fuel facility. Proper thinning and Full Vigor Forest management increases timber growth by 100% every ten years.

These timber growers have learned to make each part of the tree into its' highest value use. Small diameter logs and crooked logs and species with no commercial value have high value here. Whatever can't be made into high value products goes to the fuel storage area. Tree tops and trees removed for Timber Stand Improvement are used for fuel.

At the sawmill building, logs are efficiently sawn into lumber. One production line focuses exclusively on small diameter logs. Curved logs are common in surrounding forests and are processed with unique methods. Efficient thin kerf sawmills are quiet and safe. The low cost of modern bandsaw blades now allows the sawmilling of city trees that are notorious for containing nails, tree houses, cables, etc. that traditionally have had no commercial value.

Some wood products are sold fresh sawn, some are air dried, but most lumber is kiln dried. Solar Cycle Lumber Kilns are used to dry the boards. Solar energy is simply used to heat air to dry the wood for in-the-home high value uses. Cloudy days and night time allow the lumber to equalize the moisture content throughout the board, producing superior quality lumber compared to big commercial dry kilns.

A modern woodworking shop manufactures a variety of wood products. Solid and Natural wood Flooring, Cabinets, millwork, furniture are all simple to produce on a small scale.

Wood waste from forest management, urban forestry, and the woodworking operations is sorted into chips and fine particles. Wet chips are dried in a solar heated arch structure and piled inside at the north end. Fines are dried in another solar arch and pressed into wood fuel pellets for sale. The chips are the main biofuel used in the power plant. The wood is "gasified" then burned, generating heat and electricity. The small amount of ash is recycled back onto ag land or forest.

A separate ag-waste digester system utilizes manure and other wet waste from the area. Methane is generated and burned for heat and electricity. In the city, many sources of wet waste are available and in need of disposal. Leftover material is recycled onto ag and forest land.

Fresh Fish and Vegetables

Long greenhouses produce a steady flow of fresh food. Each day, plant seedlings are placed in floating trays at the north end of each building. Every day another tray is started and a mature tray is harvested at the other end, close to the store. Long water filled ponds each grow a different type of vegetable. A variety of fish flourish in the shared water below. Trout, tilapia, walleye, perch, bluegill, catfish are all grown. First priority is to sell fresh fish dinners at the restaurant. Excess production is sold fresh, frozen, and smoked.

The Store

All of the products made here are for sale in the retail store, plus a huge variety of locally produced items from neighboring farms. A commercial kitchen is available for area people to prepare and package local products.

The Good Food Restaurant

Three squares meals a day – all from local farms will be served in a beautiful country restaurant. Beef, pork, poultry, eggs, milk, cheese that are commonly produced all year on neighboring farms will compliment the fresh fish and vegetables grown here. Many items will be grilled on wood flames for extra flavor. Local beer and wine will be served.

Not everything will be locally grown – some things are imported for variety and pleasure. The net balance of energy, money flow, good jobs, and quality lifestyles will be very positive for the community.

The Good Food & Wood & Fuel system runs on renewable solar energy. 99% of it is collected on the surrounding hillsides and farm fields. Buildings also use solar energy for heating and lighting during the day. Wind energy is used simply for air drying wood and crops.

As the first GFWF – people from all over the world come for tours and meals and local natural products. "Old Time Lumberjack Camp" provides theme lodging for visitors and trainees that attend the "hands-on-the-job" training school. Local motels fill up and new B&Bs open all over the countryside.

None of these ideas are new – each one is a proven successful venture somewhere. What is unique is the joining of these processes into one intelligent system that produces efficiencies and higher benefits by working together. Using what is available in the local economy to meet the immediate needs of the people.

This facility makes us nearly independent of the big corporations. Our energy balance is positive, we export much more energy than we import.   We earn much more money in the local economy than we spend elsewhere.   We are again free to expand our horizons and explore the world's distant lands.

Every single community and neighborhood needs fresh food everyday.

Every single community needs wood products everywhere.

Renewable solar energy is available everywhere the sun shines

Local 'quality of life' jobs are needed for everyone.

Meaningful employment is more important than a high paying job.

There is no excuse for ignorance or selfishness today.   We Are Global – We Are In This Together.

Using "waste" wood from local trees to supply local energy needs is a Win Win for a community. Self sufficiency for a small business or community is a great insurance against disasters that likely will occur someday.

Or we can choose to just let our local wood rot and buy fossil fuel energy from the big industry.

Everyone on the planet needs to look at trees and wood in a different way – business as usual in the timber industry is bad for all of us in so many ways, while there is still time to save the remaining natural forests on our planet from corporate greed.

It is hard to change. It is devastating to learn that what you were taught is not the only way and that there may even be a much better way. We want to just be entertained and just have a party, but life is about doing the right thing for building a better life for our future.

What needs to be learned

Timber Growers and communities with trees need to see the great values that they can harvest every year from their trees to benefit their people, businesses, and communities.

Educators need to learn and teach that there is a workable and beneficial alternative to just let the huge timber corporations have their way with all of us – there is something much better than 'better than nothing'.

Our leaders need to promote the use of locally grown and manufactured wood products to build our economy with a valuable renewable resource with many benefits.

Spreading the word that there is an alternative to Industrial "sustainable forestry" is needed for every forest owner, forest manager, government worker, and educator.

The wood market situation today is the result of hundreds of years of moving away from using good local wood, to an industrial global use of highly manufactured and cheap products. We have moved from hands on knowledge of woodworking to open a printed package to get some stuff that kind of looks like wood.

There is a huge trillion dollar per year industrial system that is set in its ways and protective of itself. No one involved was around when it all come together, people today have gotten their job and adjusted into their work as how thing happen today.

The Rainforest Liquidators scandals aired on 60 Minutes over the early months of 2015 has brought a spotlight on the big industry and how far things have moved to the bad side of globalization. The company claims whatever they want on their fancy printed packaging, claiming top quality product at the cheapest price. Anyone choosing to buy cheap stuff on sale gets what they pay for.

The new power of the internet is my hope that we can make a difference here to see clearly what has happened and what can make a positive change.

Trees and wood are virtually unknown to people today and the old times skills are fading fast across the planet. Teaching people where wood product come from – that the trees right around you can be made into useful products by small business - how to do it - can bring back some common sense to our lives.

Our teachers and leaders need to see the big picture and understand that there is a workable alternative to use Good Local Wood.

Strength in numbers – the more small business the better, putting people back in control, as soon as possible
Restore the public market – local stuff for local needs on a daily basis from local business – is an old traditional method that has worked for millenia.

The local public market is the key to life in a community
The global corporate public market only benefits the tourists and a few rich cats.

The most wasteful practice we see all the time on the TV news is storm clean up – in the haste to restore power, most wood is dumped.
   Have a plan in place for using urban trees to rebuild the community and lives after a storm.
   Train workers before the storm to salvage the best value from a damaged tree. A travelling bio fuel chipper would be brought in after a storm to save the volumes of wood for use as renewable fuel.

Everything goes in cycles – up and down – over time. The wave of following the advertisements of the huge global corporations are being seen for their true effects on the planet and the people. We are returning to a more local hands on use of good wood products.

Choose to build the future with Good Local Wood instead of choosing the cheapest stuff that actually comes at a very high price to our planet.

Manage the trees around you to provide many values

There are no rules and regulations in using wood for most products – no license needed. We are free to move on this – get going under the radar and build some momentum before the corporate monsters catch on – and then use the global media and the internet to expose the corruption and bring forward change for the better for everyone.

It is no longer OK to bribe politicians and have fun with prostitutes and party to drunk extreme on trips and abuse the children &weak and have mistress and men's only clubs etc etc etc... Everything has suddenly changed and the rich and powerful men of the planet must now instantly – for the first time in history - behave in an acceptable manner.

Globalization really means we are now all in this together. It is time now to get along and compromise and work together instead of killing anyone you don't like.

This is a good thing – We need to Mature really fast here before globalization suddenly kills us all off.

Nature and the planet would go right on without us – no big deal
Nature heals and time goes on whatever.

 This is a human thing right now. We need to change – really to survive much longer.

Global Sports lets us compete and yell and scream and fight amongst countries and groups and teams, within the rules, then shake hands and go home in peace. There should be a respect in sports to do your best then go home and practice and do it all again next year.

The problem with sports is that almost everyone loses – just one wins the prize and trophy, everyone else is a loser - but then it all begins again.

Going through college in UW-Madison in the early 1970s made me a really good loser. While I was first Fluegelhorn in the Marching Band, our teams were like last place mostly. We won a game here and there, but defeat was overwhelming experience. You adapt to survive and modify your expectations.

Now Sports at UW-Madison is big business, new world!

Survival is more like we all need to win and work for the future to win again and again

Everyone is free to advertise and lie any way they want – ignorance prevails - and freedom of speech is really free. Anyone who cares needs to beware and do your research to be in control of your own life.

The Rainforest Liquidators "Chinese Made" poisonous flooring now banned - is reported already repackaged and "on sale" with nice new labeling - for anyone foolish enough to buy the cheapest wood ever from the biggest flooring corporation ever.

Our Government Programs Perpetuate the Problems

One reason that timber prices remain so low is our State foresters continue to sell public timber at very low stumpage values – to feed the timber industry and "create jobs". The State of Wisconsin is the largest timber owner in this region. Recent public timber sales in this area have sold for $3-5 per acre per year, making it very difficult for any small woodlot owner to earn a fair income. Similar conditions exist in areas where large US National Forests are present. All of this is pretty much the same across the US and the planet – the timber industry has totally been globalized.

Another obvious trend in the timber industry shows the true picture of the market today. Long ago our government gave big corporations huge tracts of land so that they could build America. The big timber corporations have now sold off most of their forest lands as they know it doesn't pay to grow trees in the global market – it is cheaper for them to get wood for a fraction of the cost of growing it - from the private landowners and government forests - who take what they can get - because it is better than nothing.

There is no hope of a fair and profitable income for a timber grower or urban forest community in the traditional market that is now become globalized. I tried everything possible for many years.

So I developed a new timber market by doing just the opposite of business as usual! There is no compromise – just choose a better way starting today.

More Forest Folly

Forest owners are told by the experts that they are not qualified to manage their own woods. Only a professional college graduate can write a forest management plan, know when a tree is mature for harvest, negotiate a market timber price for trees... Try telling that to a corn or dairy farmer!

I went to college and got my BS in Forest Science from the University of Wisconsin – Madison 1976, then learned my trees never went to college.... I do know what the foresters know. Not one forester anywhere knows what I do everyday here – they are all afraid to learn anything but the industrial logging that supports their paycheck!

In the mean-time, have patience and wait for the local market to develop rather than take what you can get today while simply feeding the big global corporations. Invest in your timber growth with the anticipation that soon there will be a good market for local wood. And work to encourage Good Local Wood businesses in your community – keep the value of your trees to build your economy. This could happened very quickly now – all the foundation has been laid and everything is ready for people to simply choose Good Local Wood.

I encourage people to manage their trees and forests, with the hope that the wood will benefit the local economy and community, not just subsidize the massive profits of a distant corporation somewhere.

Our leaders and foresters need to understand the high value of the wood products that could come from local trees. We should keep that value in the local economy instead of exporting our wood resources as cheap global commodities. Wood is something that can be easily processed by small business in the local community. Local wood is a perfect substitute for imported wood in the big box store... even better.

A lot has been done to promote the use of local food – a similar effort to encourage the use of good local wood would be a huge economic boost. People don't know much about trees or wood products anymore – "we get wood at the store".

Full Value Forestry would best practiced by a community. The producers and customers and community leaders & educators should cooperate to build the economy.

Timber is for the taking – still today

"I'm here today to make money, this is my job" - many loggers have told me this. They see all trees as their way to make money, even though the grower is not making significant or profitable income.

Cheap Wood On Sale - This likely means the stuff was made using trees that were not paid for. Most timber in the world is given to the big corporations with maybe a bribe or token payment to make it happen. Governments have always seen timber as a low value, plentiful commodity that is in the way of agriculture and progress. Giving the timber to a big corporation encourages the land to be cleared and builds the economy and puts people to work - for a while. Soon the land is ruined, industry has moved on, and the local people are left with the mess. Even if the land is farmed, ancient forest soils are soon depleted, washed away, and chemically changed by agriculture. A short term profit leads to long term environmental disaster.

Virtually all of the wood in the industrial timber market has been obtained by some measure of fraud or theft or cheating. At worst, investigative journalists from major publications have estimated many times that most of the wood used by industry is stolen or obtained by bribing the local government official. There is no significant effort or enforcement program to begin to adequately protect our global forests.

People within the industry know this is all true and the prevailing attitude is, I might as well do it too - as everyone does it, if I don't someone else will take it, and if you want to put me in jail, you will have to put everyone in jail. Loggers simply cut trees to survive in a terrible timber market – there has been no alternative – it just goes on and on. It is not the logger getting rich, they do the hard and dangerous work and are paid just enough to live on another day. It is the timber buyers, brokers, and the corporate execs that get rich off of everyone else's hard work and ignorance.

Even here in the USA where we are supposed to be "sustainable" and honest… timber is cut and sold with the same pressures around the world.

The biggest reason for the cheating is the lack of knowledge of the people who own or manage the trees. Timber has always been for the taking and all efforts for a grower or community to earn a fair income have been blocked and worn down to keep timber cheap or free for the industry.

The low value of trees and logs discourages anyone from learning about the real values of wood resources. Law enforcement agencies have too many other high priority problems to deal with, trees are not worth protecting and the landowners are left responsible for taking care of themselves. Landowners aren't paid enough to get their attention or interest, they have always just taken the occasional payment for trees as it is better than nothing.

Our State government puts timber on the market for the benefit of the sawmills and paper mills at the expense of the local timber growers and communities. Around SW Wisconsin, the State is the largest forest owner by far and puts timber up for sale at ridiculously low prices that benefit loggers and mills from up North – hundreds of miles away. Selling at give-away prices sets a precedent in the market that makes it very difficult for any woodlot owner to ever get a better value for their trees.

About the worst situation of all is in our local School Forest. The pine plantations have never had much value, so no one pays much attention. The State foresters set up harvests at low prices for the industry from up North and no one in the Schools even knows what is happening – they just trust the State to take care of them with what little income might come their way. The values are so low, no one even bothers to count the number of truck loads hauled away or what values are paid for what trees. A recent sale of pine in the School forest was valued at $17 per ton, but no one local even knows what went to the paper mill and what logs were sold at higher value to sawmills or how many truck loads were actually taken. The income to the School was reported at about $3 per acre per year, but no one really cares. Everyone is taught over and over that trees are not worth owning or growing or harvesting – the logs are all hauled hundreds of miles away by someone – no one really knows or cares.

Even in the best of the best situations in timber sales on private lands here, where the landowners are likely among the most informed in the world – the bias of a timber buyer and "professional" forester shortchanges the timber grower in many ways.

The price of timber has nothing to do with the value of the wood – the market price for trees is based on supply and demand, but in a perverted way due to the discrepancy in the level of knowledge between the buyers and wood sellers. Since no one knows significant information on logs and values, the buyers dominate the sellers. The buyer is in command and the individual seller is at the mercy of a huge corporate secret system. Timber buyers have told me that it gets kind of boring dealing with ignorant landowners and they have created a kind of 'Sport' of timber buying to entertain themselves. I could write a whole book on the crazy corrupt timber markets in S Wisconsin that I have been involved with. Now I just choose to avoid it all completely, and I advise others that they could find a better way!

In 40 years in the Wisconsin Timber Industry – the most striking thing in my mind is the difference in the way I think and act when I'm a timber buyer - as opposed to when I'm the timber seller. I hate myself when I'm in the position to buy wood. My bias and behavior is the opposite of when I'm selling wood. The knowledge factor is so obvious but why should I pay a fair price when everyone else is bidding following all the rules of the game of buying trees.

The real answer for our planet is to develop and support community based cooperative businesses to effectively use our good local wood and local food and renewable biofuel resources. Our efforts to start the Sustainable Woods Cooperative system has been blocked and sidetracked by the professional foresters who feel they need to keep the forest owners under their control – keep the "sheeple" quiet & content in their huge flocks until it is the landowners turn to feed the appetite of the huge timber industry.

When I opened my Timber Growers store in 2007, we did four harvests with other forest owners in the area. I paid them 2 to 4 times above market price and showed that we all made money. Everyone wants more money, but it was disappointing no one was willing to get involved for even that level of payment.

All of our efforts here in Wisconsin the past 40 years to organize and educate and empower the forest owners, The Wisconsin Woodland Owners Association and The Sustainable Woods Cooperatives…. were taken over by the government foresters, Universities, and industry with the money and power to block all efforts of landowners to have a profitable and informed business as timber growers.

Despite being the most abundant agricultural crop in our State, the management of our timber is disgraceful compared to any other crop, and that is due to a long standing effort to keep landowners ignorant, so they just obediently feed the timber industry in their turn.

Trophy timber – choosing to use rare and exotic wood – encourages illegal logging of natural forests. We have learned to scorn the use of Trophy Animals, rare trees are important to the planet also. Taking just the scattered high value trees from a forest also does serious long term damage.

The High Cost of Cheap Wood

If wood is cheap – you have to understand that it was taken without benefiting the local community, rather to their long term detriment.

Once the trees have been cut down and removed, cheap wood most likely was processed in Asia where the costs of labor are kept very low. Wages are minimal and worker safety is of little concern. Environmental protection is ignored in the effort to minimize expenses to that the wood products are as cheap as possible. Old technology using poisonous materials, glues, and finishes are used to make cheap stuff that soon is worn out and must be replaced. Raw wood is shipped around the world for cheap processing, then finished products are shipped again to population centers. Modern packaging and labeling makes any claim of responsibility or origin look legitimate – customers just want to see a printed assurance. Monitoring wood products sales is insignificant in the global market.

Fortunately for our small local timber growing business – real wood products do have high value in the retail markets. For most wood products - 99%+ of the retail price goes to the manufacturers, shippers, middlemen, and retailers after paying the timber grower next to nothing for the trees. Our business cuts out all the middlemen and connects our forest directly with the wood customer. Earning all of the money of wood products allows our small business to survive in a global market of monster corporations.

If you buy local wood – your money stays in the local economy and builds the community.

If you buy imported wood – your money is exported and the local economy is neglected and worn down.

We all want to think that buying a lot of cheap stuff will give us a better way of life – we want to be fooled that saving a little money is better.

Cheap wood products are a prime example of the real picture in the world today:

For a company to sell stuff at the lowest price – they obviously have to cut every corner possible, abusing the people and planet with no excuse but greed, and using the cheapest workers in their stores too.

Our leaders and teachers are so wrapped up in the money of the big global corporations, they no longer lead us in ways that benefit our local economy. All of this is so bizarre and unbelievable and sad and scandalous and disgraceful – I won't and don't have any dealings in the timber industry or forestry profession any longer. This is all why I developed a separate timber market for our annual harvest of wood products. All I can say is that anyone who deals in the big industrial timber markets – beware the monsters! It is up to wood customers to choose their future on our planet.

Rescue tools that I use on the Fire Department have changed in 35 years – forestry hasn't much.

Everyday I answer the same old questions from people about flooring – 100 year old myths still rule – my Dad did it, Grandpa did it, everyone does it, so we do it here.

www.ingramcontent.com/pod-product-compliance
Lightning Source LLC
Chambersburg PA
CBHW050756180526
45159CB00003B/1485